Celebrating Time Alone
Stories of Splendid Solitude

Lionel Fisher

Celebrating Time Alone

Stories of Splendid Solitude

Lionel Fisher

BEYOND
WORDS
Publishing

Beyond Words Publishing. Inc.
20827 N.W. Cornell Road. Suite 500
Hillsboro. Oregon 97124-9808
503-531-8700
1-800-284-9673

Editor: Rosemary Wray
Copyeditor: David Abel
Proofreaders: David Abel and Michael Ashby
Design: Principia Graphica and Dorral Lukas
Composition: William H. Brunson Typography Services
Managing editor: Julie Steigerwaldt

Printed in the United States of America
Distributed to the book trade by Publishers Group West

Library of Congress Cataloging-in-Publication Data

Fisher. Lionel L.
    Celebrating time alone : stories of splendid solitude / Lionel Fisher.
        p. cm.
    ISBN 1-58270-049-4 (pbk.) ISBN 978-1-58270-049-6
        1. Solitude.   I. Title.

BF637.S64 F57   2001
155.9'2—dc21

                                    00-068078

The corporate mission of Beyond Words Publishing. Inc.:
    Inspire to Integrity

To new life, fresh hope:
For Sophie, born April 8, 2000

Contents

Chapter One   1

Finding a Path with Heart: The New Hermits

Living alone, the new millennium's predominant lifestyle.
Overcoming the onus, going against the grain, tasting
the silence, vital explorations, restructured priorities,
assuming the awesome responsibility for ourselves.
Susan's basic life, Ed's private passions, Ric's patient wait,
William's relinquished burden.

Chapter Two   19

Gone to Innisfree: Journey to the Undiscovered Country

A six-year retreat at the beach, the dizziness of freedom, essential
confrontations, vital answers, a separate peace. Daring
aloneness, surviving the memories, trusting the stillness.
In search of God, meaning, self, the real American Dream.
Deconstructing, reinventing, recouping passion, being wise in
time, a final reckoning, Ann's "Terrors of a Woman Alone."

Acknowledgments

For a long time, I was the only one who believed in this book. Then, one by one, these special people came to believe as well; to them I extend my sincere appreciation, affection, and gratitude:

My agent, the wonderful Susan Travis of Burbank, California. What a delightful phrase, "my agent," as in "My agent says ... I couldn't have done it without my agent.... My agent is *terrific!*"

The patient, perceptive, perspicacious editors at Beyond Words Publishing: Rosemary Wray, for whom the proposal "resonated," and whose firm, sensitive hand was later vital in shaping a leaner, stronger, consistently honest book. The ever obliging, unfailingly helpful Julie Steigerwaldt. The highly creative, thoroughly professional Laura Carlsmith. Copyeditor David Abel, who did what he had to do while treating the highly personal thoughts and feelings with integrity and respect. And at the top where all decisions stop and start, the kind, open, gutsy Cindy Black. I'm glad I don't have to call a publisher if my house catches fire, but I can't imagine a more capable, inspiring crew to put out a book.

The Contessas of Portland: Carene, who encouraged me to approach Beyond Words as the perfect publisher for this book—had she not, it might have stayed in my head and heart forever; and Janet, whose huge enthusiasm and participation have proven indispensable to its scope and integrity.

Joleen Colombo, whose encouragement for me to record my odyssey to the beach in *Writers NW* sowed the seeds for this book.

Jane, who has shared my life through all the years together and apart, who knows me better and cares for me more than anyone save our children, and for whom many of the unspoken apologies and acknowledged regrets in this book are intended.

And all of the generous, unselfish men and women who shared with me their thoughts, feelings, heartfelt emotions, and unflinching honesty. Without their inspiring words and courageous stories, there would be no book. You know who you are.

Preface

We write alone, but we do not
write in isolation. No matter how
fantastic a story line may be, it
still comes out of our response
to what is happening to us and
to the world in which we live.
—MADELEINE L'ENGLE

This is a book of stories. The people in the stories are real; what they tell of their lives is true.

Their truths may not be your truths. The choices they have made you might shun. The paths they have traveled may stray far from your own. Then again, some of their truths, some of their paths could become yours.

These courageous men and women have told their stories, revealed their struggles, heartaches, failures, and successes—not for the judgment of others, but for their own sake and for their own validation: to understand, confirm, and celebrate the marvelous discovery of themselves.

It is because of them that this book does not contain the usual Greek chorus of professional healers proclaiming yea or nay, this isn't normal, this isn't right.

If part of their longing, pain, triumph, and redemption touches some-thing inside of you and helps you to find your own answers, your own paths, your own fulfillment, then that is reason enough to share them.

Introduction

solitaire ... *a precious stone,*
esp. a diamond, set by itself.

It scares us more than anything except death.

Being alone.

Our fear of aloneness is so ingrained that given the choice of being by ourselves or being with others we opt for safety in numbers, even at the expense of lingering in painful, boring, or totally unredeeming company.

And yet more of us than ever *are* alone.

While many Americans have their solo lifestyles thrust on them—people die, people go away—a huge and growing population is *choosing* to be alone.

In 1955, one in ten U.S. households consisted of one person. By 1999, the proportion was one in three. Single men

> *"Never before in American history has living alone been the predominant lifestyle."*

and women accounted for 38.9 million of the nation's 110.5 million households. Sixty percent of them were under the age of sixty-five; roughly 60 percent of them were women.

On the cusp of the new century, approximately 14.3 million American women and 24.6 million American men over the age of twenty-five lived alone, according to the U.S. Census Bureau.

By 1999, single parents with children under the age of eighteen made up 27.3 percent of the nation's 70.9 million family households. Among them were 2.1 million father-child and 9.8 million mother-child families. Forty-two percent of single-parent mothers had never wed.

Meanwhile, many more Americans are divorcing. In less than three decades, reports the Census Bureau, the number of divorced men and women has more than quadrupled—to a total of 18.3 million in 1996, compared to 4.3 million in 1970.

And many more Americans are not marrying. The number of adult men and women who have remained single has more than doubled in thirty years—to 44.9 million in 1996 from 21.4 million in 1970.

"Never before in American history has living alone been the predominant lifestyle," observes demographic trends analyst Cheryl Russell, who predicts that single-person households will become the most common household type in the United States by the year 2005.

Nonetheless, we persist in the conviction that a solitary existence is the harshest penalty life can mete out. We loathe being alone—anytime, anywhere, for too long, for whatever reason.

From childhood we're conditioned to accept that when alone we instinctively ache for company, that loners are outsiders yearning to get in rather than people who are content with their own company.

Alone, we squander life by rejecting its full potential and wasting its remaining promises. Alone, we accept that experiences unshared are barely worthwhile, that sunsets viewed singly are not as spectacular, that time spent apart is fallow and pointless.

And so we grow old believing we are nothing by ourselves, steadfastly shunning the opportunities for self-discovery and personal growth that solitude could bring us.

We've even coined a word for those who prefer to be by themselves: *antisocial*, as if they were enemies of society. They are viewed as friendless, suspect in a world that goes around in twos or more and is wary of solitary travelers.

People who need people are threatened by people who don't. The idea of seeking contentment alone is heretical, for society steadfastly decrees that our completeness lies in others.

Instead, we cling to each other for solace, comfort, and safety, believing that we are nothing alone—insignificant, unfulfilled, lost—accepting solitude in the tiniest, most reluctant of slices, if at all, which is tragic, for it rejects God's precious gift of life.

Ironically, most of us crave more intimacy and companionship than we can bear. We begrudge ourselves, our spouses, and our partners sufficient physical and emotional breathing room, and then bemoan the suffocation of our relationships.

To point out these facts is not to suggest we should abandon all our close ties. Medical surveys show that the majority of elderly people who live alone, yet maintain frequent contact with relatives and friends, rate their physical and emotional well-being as "excellent." Just as an apple a day kept the doctor away when they were young, an active social calendar appears to serve the same purpose now.

But we need to befriend and enjoy *ourselves* as well.

How does that old song go? "I've been to paradise, but I've never been to me...."

"We must relearn to be alone," exhorts Anne Morrow Lindbergh in her inspirational book, *Gift from the Sea*. "Instead of planting our solitude with dream blossoms, we choke the space with continuous music, chatter, and companionship to which we do not even listen. It is simply there to fill the vacuum."

"We can't stand the silence," said Agnes de Mille, "because silence includes thinking. And if we thought, we would have to face ourselves."

Let us learn, then, from those in search of what they have not been able to find and hold in the press of humanity around them: peace of mind, gentleness of heart, calmness of spirit, daily joy. Those who are mastering the art of flying solo and soaring to their highest human potential.

Who have come to understand that to know and to love and to be of value to others, they first must know and love and value themselves; that to find their way in the world, they have to start by finding themselves.

"Before we can surrender ourselves we must *become* ourselves," Thomas Merton pointed out. "For no one can give up what he does not possess."

They are the men and women who have found nobility in turning to themselves first when facing life's challenges—and not blaming anyone else if they fail.

Who find silence eloquent rather than empty.

Who have discovered that being alone can impose a startling clarity in their lives, achieved through the personal reflection we seem to allow ourselves only in times of severe loss and intense grief.

Who trust their aloneness, using it to embrace and nurture their individuality, to celebrate themselves in their own special ways.

Who have become boon companions to the best friends they'll ever have. Guess who?

Who are living alone well, even magnificently, in full affirmation of the preciousness of life.

The premise of this book is timeless and simple: there are gifts we can only give ourselves, lessons no one else can teach us, triumphs we must achieve alone.

It affirms that it is all right to be alone, to *want* to be alone, to be alone and not lonely—even to be lonely at times—because the rewards of solitude are worth the deprivations.

It sings the triumphs of those who have found amazing grace alone.

Their inspirational stories and messages of hope are filled with the resilience, courage, and strength of people who deal gracefully, even heroically, with life—even if it isn't the life they wanted—because not to do so would be a repudiation of life itself.

They lead us in quest of our own undiscovered selves.

To follow them, we must be willing to do what frightens us most. Be alone.

Unbuckle the yoke, drop the load, turn down the volume. Be still.

And *listen*.

Above all, we must hail the silence.

Chapter One

Finding a Path with Heart:
The New Hermits

Let silence in.
She will rarely speak or mew.
She will sleep on my bed
And all I have ever been
Either false or true
Will live again in my head.
—MAY SARTON

In the spring of 1996, Sarah Holbrook moved to a place as basic as the life she wants to live.

A forty-four-year-old entrepreneur who had parlayed her intelligence, charm, and wit into an annual income approaching six figures, she sold her house and flourishing business in a major city to purchase six acres and a 15′ × 30′ cabin in a remote valley of Washington's rugged Cascade Mountains.

Here the middle child of an English family of three boys and two girls, all born in the same house on Trollope Street in a working-class neighborhood of London, went to ground, so to speak.

Her new home is thick with maple and soaring fir—though the previous owners had logged some of the timber, leaving shorn roots and torn branches bulldozed into muddy piles. A recent windstorm brought down eight more trees, which she will have to clear as well.

"The place is a mess," she observes ruefully. "But I loved it the moment I saw it."

The cabin has a loft across its midriff, says the twice-divorced mother of a grown son, now on his own and living across the country. The roof was built with a steep pitch to handle the winter snows; she's able to stand upright only in the center of the lone, sprawling room.

The structure has no foundation; it was erected on concrete posts that are sinking into the earth, and she'll have to jack up the cabin to lay in a foundation. There is no kitchen; she draws cold water from a well tapped by a pressure tank. There is no bathroom; she's installed a composting toilet shipped to her from a manufacturer in Maine.

"But there *is* electricity," she says with a grin.

An emerald forest embracing a bountiful garden beside a snug cottage garlanded with bright shutters and, inside, yards of white lace and flowery fabrics. This is what Holbrook envisions when the monumental work is done.

"I will take care of this place," she vows softly. "And it will take care of me."

I ask the inevitable question, one she's no doubt heard endlessly from family and friends: "Why?" In the prime of her life, why has she come to this reclusive place, alone?

Holbrook is silent for a while, choosing the exact words to articulate reasons she's probably given many times before—to convince herself, I sense, more than others.

"My dream is to live in peace and dignity," she says finally.

"To respect nature and explore the creative side of my humanness. Here I can make my own mistakes. I won't mind making them because they'll be *my* mistakes. And I'll learn from them."

Another pause, then, "I don't even mind the work, which is pretty daunting, but I'll handle it."

Will she get someone to help her? The answer is curt. "Someone else would just take over." I picture John Wayne striding up, the distinctive list to starboard, standing there, arms akimbo, competent, assured: "Move over, little lady, I'll handle this."

I know exactly what she means, but Holbrook drives home her point anyway: "Whatever I built here wouldn't be mine anymore."

She shrugs, grimaces, runs quick fingers through black hair besieged by gray. When she speaks again her voice is gentle, the hazel eyes have softened.

"Most of my life has been spent trying to earn other people's esteem, their approval, starting with my mother. Now this place is *mine*. This place and this life. I own them completely. I've come to realize no man is going to rescue me, that I need to make my own future secure. No one is going to do it for me. I've decided I need to be self-sustaining, that I can't rely on anyone but myself, and this is a good way to be."

"I'll live in harmony with the seasons, be kind to my environment, be energy-efficient, try not to waste, not to pollute. I'll live simply, have less stuff, do what I love—sew, tend my garden, learn, build things, be quiet, maybe even become serene one day."

> "Once you accept your aloneness, once you face it and quit being scared, it becomes like a wonderful secret you learn. Then you know it can't hurt you. Then it becomes precious."

She lapses into silence once more. Then says softly, "I can grow old here without feeling the need to be young and beautiful."

What about physical intimacy? The question brings a chuckle. "I miss it, of course," Holbrook replies.

"I still wonder if I'll meet a man someday who'll be *the* one, as they say. There's a sadness I sometimes feel—that I won't have another romantic love. But I'm not really hopeful."

Holbrook laughs. "It's just as well since I'm not very good at picking mates. In the past I've chosen men with addictive problems and huge attitudes. And I've always had trouble with people telling me what to do."

She laughs again. "Sure, I miss the sex. Growing up in the sixties I was openly sexual. I'm a highly sexual person, always have been. Now, nearing menopause, I'm losing out on the best sex of my life."

And that's all right with her? "Sure," she snaps the word back. "If it means taking care of my other priorities right now."

Is she afraid of being lonely?

"I was at first," Holbrook replies. "But once you accept your aloneness, once you face it and quit being scared, it becomes like a wonderful secret you learn. Then you know it can't hurt you. Then it becomes precious."

Unlike Sarah Holbrook, Ed Sorenson has always known that he wanted to be alone.

Since leaving home at the age of seventeen, he has lived in urban seclusion. A personable forty-year-old intellectual who is as comfortable quoting London, Conrad, and Heller as Pascal, Schiller, and Camus, Sorenson has structured his life to safeguard his solitude, both at home and at work.

Despite possessing a bachelor's degree in psychology and a master's in economics, he works the night shift as a security guard in a metropolitan office building. It's the occupation he chose fourteen years ago. "There aren't many jobs in the city where you can work alone," he explains.

Sorenson had just two prerequisites for his employment. First, he wouldn't have to deal with people. Second, he'd be able to read, sleep, and "space out" on the job.

A diligent employee, he's been offered promotions to security management and has turned them all down, along with opportunities to transfer to the day shift. He is, he says, perfectly content with the way things are.

Sorenson did accept one management position several years ago, he reveals. "It taught me a lot about people and about myself—enough to turn down any further promotions and to quit working full time."

Doing what he does, he can read, write, contemplate, compose music, practice his dance steps (he's an accomplished ballroom dancer), even sing out loud, he says. "The time is completely my own. Best of all, I don't have to bother with anyone else. I don't think I'm missing much by being out of the mainstream."

He guards his solitude just as zealously at home. A classical and jazz pianist who entertains at public and private functions, his first priority is his music. He practices at his piano a minimum of three hours each day in the basement apartment he rents in a private home in a large Western city. His second passion is reading, an insatiable, lifelong habit.

He bicycles to and from work. And he cuts his own hair. "Why depend on someone else for anything you're perfectly capable of doing yourself?"

He didn't own an answering machine until a friend convinced him it wasn't polite not to provide a way for people to reach him, particularly because he seldom answers his phone when he is home.

But the tall, lanky outdoors enthusiast is adamant about not owning a car, content to haul his backpack and inflatable kayak by bus whenever he chooses to indulge another passion: exploring the rivers and forests of the Pacific Northwest—by himself.

"I most enjoy the things I can do alone," he says matter-of-factly. "And the *last* place I want to be with anyone is in nature."

Sorenson traces his affinity for being alone to an unhappy childhood. "I didn't like my family," he admits candidly. "I wasn't treated kindly by them. We're on better terms now, but as a boy I didn't feel safe or loved. I preferred to be alone—reading or exploring in the woods or playing the piano."

His distrust of others was heightened by his experiences in school, he adds. The outcome was predictable. "Only alone," he says, "do I really feel at ease."

It's also why he vacations by himself. Sorenson spent three weeks in Belize recently, snorkeling and trekking the Mayan ruins. Two friends asked to come along, he reveals, but he turned them down.

"When I travel I don't like to compromise where I go and what I do," he explains. "With no one else to consider, I can indulge myself completely."

Isn't that selfish of him?

He laughs out loud, as if I'd told a joke. "Well, yes, I suppose it is," Sorenson replies. "But I prefer to use the term 'self-indulgent.' Look it up. It means yielding to one's own pleasures, whims, and desires, without restraint or modification. I see nothing wrong with that."

When he's in a new and exciting place, Sorenson says, time is even more precious. "The moments become intense, each day is long and lingering. It's as if time slows palpably. It's an uncanny feeling."

He's certain that the sensation results from focusing so intently on whatever pleasures him that his enjoyment literally stretches the minutes and hours.

"Talk interferes with sensuality," he says. "When conversation turns banal, I feel a sense of deprivation. Solitude shuts down our cognitive functions and allows us to *feel* what we're experiencing. Other people are superfluous to the sensual experience. In fact, they're detrimental."

What about sex?

He laughs again. "What's that?"

Actually. Sorenson says, he could have more than his share of sex but isn't willing to pay the price. I ask, "What price is that?" He replies, "What most people want, which is first call to as much of their partner's time, attention, energy, and emotion as they need. That's incompatible with how I prefer to live my life, which involves devoting a maximum amount of time to my music, to my reading, and to my hobbies—whatever's most important to me at the moment."

> "The way to be happy is to develop an unshakable sense of worth in yourself."

How about a purely physical relationship? "There's no such thing," he retorts. "It would be like finding a unicorn, delightful but highly improbable." Sorenson is visibly amused by the notion.

"There is no free sex," he repeats emphatically. "Not for the man, not for the woman. One or the other always pays, mostly with the games people play with each other. The games always follow. There's no sex without the games, without the bullshit. We all want to feel cherished, safe, and important," he concedes.

"Men tend to do it with work, women with relationships. But romantic involvements aren't the answer. They never make us feel as secure or worthwhile or as important as we'd like, and not for very long. The way to be happy is to develop an unshakable sense of worth in yourself," he concludes.

"That way you don't have to rely on anyone else for your security and contentment. When you find it yourself, no one can take it away from you. Only *you* can."

Four years after we first talked, I phoned Sorenson to ask him if anything had changed in his life. "I've had two encounters with women for whom I felt love," he replied.

"As a result, I realized there was a part of me that *did* long for the pleasures of being a husband and father. When I was younger, I intuitively realized my inadequacy in this regard, and I denied and suppressed these longings. Later, upon being rejected, and not unreasonably so, I became seriously depressed and reevaluated my desires and disposition toward the life I'd chosen.

"I had to face the fact that I couldn't adapt to the mainstream world of work and the level of sociability needed to be a successful husband and father, that it was too late for me, that each of us has to live in the world we create for ourselves, that my disposition was my fate and I had to make the most of it.

"For me, that means living alone, as I've done my entire life."

———————

Most Americans wouldn't agree. Nor understand. And certainly not sympathize.

They'd shake their heads in disapproval and say that Holbrook, the successful entrepreneur ensconced in her reclusive cabin, had found her American Dream of material success and social acceptance. Then threw it away. And for what? Withdrawal, isolation, loneliness!

They'd accuse Sorenson of never having pursued the dream, miring himself instead in estrangement, disgruntlement, and failure.

Call them the new hermits.

In greater and greater numbers, they are going against the grain of society, deliberately out of step with the march of life around them, consciously out of sync with the ordained way of doing things.

Like the desert fathers of old, who were the rebels of their time, they are foregoing common ground for individual paths in search of their own destinies.

They were the early ones, notes Benedicta Ward, who broke the rules of the world. "Their name itself, anchorite, means rule-breaker, the one who does not fulfill his public duties."

The new hermits are modern men and women of all ages, in all walks of life, driven by a fierce need for self-actualization, daring to venture into deserts of their own making.

Having pursued the American Dream, they have come closer than any previous generation to being perfect parents, perfect coworkers, perfect neighbors, perfect friends. Some achieved wealth, status, even fame in the process, only to find that it wasn't enough because they'd lost sight of who they were and the preciousness of the ordinary.

Having kept faith with conventional wisdom, they found it wanting. No longer consumed by practical considerations and manifestations of success, they are attempting to bring real meaning and passion back into their lives.

For them, time spent alone, away from the soul-robbing demands of everyday living, has become crucial to understanding their true selves, their reasons for being, and their pertinence to God, themselves, and the world.

And they are found everywhere. Rock stars, certainly, aren't noted for making inward journeys, but John Frusciante is grateful for his. "I spent six years going inside myself in a way that people who are stuck with the idea that they have to accomplish something with their lives never got a chance to do," said the guitarist for the Red Hot Chili Peppers.

"The scariest thing," notes Kansas writer Laura Wexler, "is that for the first time I know no one can decide anything for me but me. Because no one knows what I know about myself."

Ric Cengeri doesn't know when or even *if* he ever made a conscious decision to be a solitary person. He does know that from a very young age he was much more independent than his brothers and sister and the other kids in the neighborhood. "I'd hop on my bike and ride into the next town to see where the road would lead me," says the forty-year-old Miami advertising agency executive.

"Usually I'd wind up watching a sporting event I came across, and at times even got invited to umpire or play," reveals the former college instructor, publications director, copy editor, and radio disc jockey. "But participation wasn't the goal. Observing life outside of my own little cocoon was the quest and the reward. My interests in music, sports, geography, culture, and others—there were so many—always ran to the obscure. While other kids were wrapped up in baseball, I pushed further and wanted to know about cricket. Or jaialai. Or shinty."

"While my classmates were content learning the state capitals, I wanted to know the cities and towns of Scotland and Iceland. And while others found companionship with the opposite sex to be the ultimate achievement, I was content for that to happen as life unfolded—in its natural time and place.

"As one continues down the solitary path, I discovered, one doesn't have to be antisocial. I consider myself one of the most social beings I know. But at the end of the day, I've found, the solitary individual can retire to his own space and be at peace, to recuperate from the day's rigors, to enjoy the special world he's built for himself."

There are two kinds of people in the world, Cengeri believes. There are the vast majority who fear loneliness and make whatever compromises necessary to avoid it, who would rather be with someone—*anyone*—than be alone. And there are those who would rather spend time with themselves in order to get to know and understand and become comfortable with who *they* are.

He has long been aware, Cengeri says, that he has always been part of this second, much smaller group. "These are the people who enjoy being by themselves, who don't need to be with others to feel actualized, who relish their solitude—the freedom, openness, and nonconformity it brings to their lives. Is one type of person right and the other wrong?" he asks rhetorically, then quickly answers himself, "No. Does one have a choice between becoming one or the other? Probably not."

"Can one learn to switch sides, as it were, if one were unhappy and had a deep-seated desire to do so? Yes, of course, and many resolutely try their whole lives to remain a part of that overwhelming majority of the blissfully commingled."

It's not hard to see why so-called loners compose the minority of society, Cengeri points out. "The world isn't really designed for single people, much the way it isn't tailored to left-handers. It's a world for righties that makes lefties adjust accordingly. But if one accepts his destiny as a loner—even a left-handed loner," he adds with a slight grin, "simply taking life in stride, facing it squarely and unflinchingly, never shunning the world as it comes to him, then his can be as rich and full a life as anyone's."

As it became more and more evident that he stood a good chance of spending most, if not all, of his life alone—without a spouse or family, that is—Cengeri made two very important decisions. "The first," he says, "was that I would *never* compromise my standards merely to avoid living a solitary life."

"My friends couldn't understand why I wouldn't want to have someone with me to avoid growing old by myself—to face what they believed would be a lonely life for me simply because I was alone. I've always been alone, but I've also always had enough friends and loved ones to call upon—so why would they all abandon me in my old age? I've asked others this question: 'If I could guarantee that you would *definitely* meet the love of your life—the one person, above all others, who was meant for *you*—would you wait until you were eighty-eight, if necessary, to meet that person?'

"They all said no. Well, I'm nearing the halfway mark to eighty-eight. And I still say I'm willing to wait that long if I have to, but I won't compromise."

His second decision, says Cengeri, was that he would never forego doing anything he wanted to do simply because he had to do it alone.

"When I think of all the great experiences I've had that I'd have missed out on if I'd waited until I had someone else to do them with, my life would be so lacking. Trips to Canada and Scotland would have been missed. Wonderful films would have gone unviewed. Delicious food would have gone untasted. I'm not trying to discount how wonderful shared experiences can be," Cengeri adds.

"Not by any stretch. But I *am* saying that when life deals you a certain hand, you need to play it for all it's worth. If you fold before playing your hand out, you never know if you would have won."

Another thing people think he's missed out on is having children, Cengeri says: "Someone to carry on my name and, again, to look after me when I'm old. True, I've bypassed that option of my life. But I've had the opportunity to teach on the college level, and I have almost a hundred former students with whom I maintain a type of parent-child bond—one, I think, that will continue for the rest of our lives."

"I've offered these youngsters my help and my guidance for as long as they need it. I've always said that if I could sell that guidance, I'd be a very rich man. Come to think of it, I *am* a rich man. If all I ever turn out to be is a 'catcher in the rye'—that critical person pointing unsuspecting people away from the cliff—then I think I will have succeeded handsomely in a very noble profession."

"I'm more than ever of the opinion that a decent human existence is possible only on the fringes of society."

These are Hannah Arendt's words, says Emily Farrell, sixty-eight, who offers them at the outset of our discussion on new hermits.

"Many of them, I'm sure, wish they could connect to others," says Farrell, a retired college instructor and grandmother, who has lived alone since her divorce fifteen years ago. "But they've never learned how, or perhaps are rejecting common values, having found them unfulfilling and superficial. So they seek their own inner voices instead, to diffuse or soften or tune out the noises of the world. I'm full of questions—where to start? How do new hermits finally connect," she asks, "when connection—belonging—becomes part of their longing? How, if they've never learned to filter out the discordance except through separateness? And is this distancing merely a form of egotism? Modern society overstimulates our senses," Farrell stresses.

"It drowns out reason and dictates our feelings, while robbing us of the critical time we need to quietly sit and synthesize our own experiences, to recognize what fits and what doesn't, what needs to be nurtured, what has to be rejected."

"Yet we also need togetherness—family, friends, community," she concedes, "because we can't distinguish uniqueness until we know sameness. And since we can't experience *everything*, we must profit and grow from the experiences of others, from their successes and failures, from their individual ways. We are, indeed, inheritors of the 'collective unconscious,' as Jung suggests."

"What others have invented we don't have to reinvent. What they've built, what they've written, we can learn from. In this way we are interdependent—not abjectly dependent or aloofly independent but simply reliant on each other.

"If humans were condemned from birth to constantly start over, like the caveman, to invest their entire existence honing and implementing their survival skills, the species would have disappeared from the earth a long time ago.

"Over the ages, though, many have had the privilege of taking time from basic survival to make the world more closely resemble a place for the spirit to soar—to give voice to our better selves—to raise the horizons of our dreams and aspirations, to examine, articulate, and advance the human condition.

"Most of these creative spirits, no doubt, have had to disengage from the ordinary, to seek solitude in an attempt to distill their philosophies.

"But most of the world has turned away from a desire for contemplation to a need for entertainment. Modern society has become mass culture: noisy, distracting, unsettling, way too fast. We need to be *doing*—to serve and be served in order to feel we're achieving, accomplishing, succeeding.

"Solitude is not valued and, in fact, is disdained because it doesn't result in a tangible, salable product. It isn't productive, doesn't benefit the economy." Not by choice but by circumstance has she become a new hermit, says Farrell.

"I now constantly question myself and the world, weighing what I believe against conventional wisdom—how obnoxious so late in the game! Asking oneself what's important takes intelligence and will, because we've been conditioned to press on mindlessly, be part of the norm, run with the pack. Following anointed paths is safe and comforting because we can do it without thinking. We can point fingers at those who seek to be different, who *are* different, who've shouted: 'Stop! Look! Listen a while.' So it can be 'crazy-making' for those who stand apart from the crowd, who try to find their own way, seek to balance what's going on inside them with what's happening in the world outside," Farrell continues.

"Unless we achieve some healthy accommodation to that outside world, unless we reach some peace with ourselves and others, unless we come to value and feel safe in honoring what others have learned about their individuality, we can become asocial or psychopathic or egotistical in our quest to distinguish ourselves from the species."

"New hermits need to be their own heroes, men and women of deliberation and action, but also, by instinct, poets, strivers toward the ideal, synthesizers of all that is best in *being*, preferably within but, if necessary, beyond the vale of common human experience. I'm only just beginning to develop a philosophy for the rest of my life," Farrell concludes.

"I'm still a 'work in progress.' But this I do believe: that though I must be mindful of the past, I must not project it on the future. Good and bad things will continue to happen to me, for this is simply life. But I will no longer expect failure, and I will accept the triumphs, not as accidents, but as my due, for I will have earned them."

———————————

"Accountability" is the word William Carrington, sixty-five, uses to explain his contentment with the solitude in his life right now. "Perhaps for the first time ever, I am no longer accountable to anyone," he says. "This is the major component of my serenity."

Raised by a deaf mother and father, Carrington learned early about the heavy yoke of duty and dependency. "My entire childhood," he relates, "was spent in the 'service' of my parents. In many ways, I considered myself totally accountable for their welfare. From my earliest recollections, I felt responsible for making sure only good things happened to them, that they got all the rights and privileges 'normal' people get. I felt that if anything bad befell them, it would in some way be my fault, either because I wasn't there at the particular moment they needed me, or they didn't get the 'message' in sign language from me in time, or they misunderstood it because I hadn't conveyed it properly."

"But it was always my fault—at least that's how I felt—because my filial duty was to function as their 'ears' and connection to the world. Therefore, it was incumbent on me to measure up each and every time they needed me so they would never suffer or miss out, at least that's how I felt. Do you know the enormous burden that places on a child?" Carrington falls silent. Nearly a minute passes before he answers his own question.

"I do. I know, in a sense, that I never had a childhood. From as young as I can remember, I was primarily my parents' 'ears.' Every time Dad had to take the car to the garage, every time Mom had to go to the dentist, every time they both had to go to the IRS to have their taxes done, every time Mom had to go shopping for clothes, whether it was for a new hat or a new corset—this was back in the forties—every time we all went out to eat in a restaurant, every time my folks had to go to the bank, to see the lawyer or the insurance agent or the doctor, every time the plumber came, every time we went to trade in the old car for a new one, every time we went on an auto trip, William was pulled from whatever he was doing to go along and be the interpreter.

"I remember feeling like a physical appendage to my parents, since they never went anywhere without me. And probably far more important, from a psychological standpoint, I always felt very, very responsible for them, as if it was up to me to make sure they got safely through life because they couldn't do it on their own. Now what could be more wacky for a little kid?

"Their way of summoning me was to step outside and clap their hands loudly; when I'd hear the clapping, no matter what I was doing, I'd head for home. I knew I was 'needed,' that someone had come to the house and was asking them questions or they were heading out on an errand and needed me to 'talk' for them. This all began, mind you, back before I even started the first grade and continued through high school."

This feeling of accountability—to parents, to family, to church, to community, to employers, to all the deaf people who came to depend on him—persisted throughout his adulthood, Carrington says. He married early, days after his nineteenth birthday, and became the parent of the first of three children at the age of twenty-one.

After his divorce he entered into relationships he regrets, hooking up with people who had problems such as alcoholism and insolvency. "I fell into the trap of feeling accountable to them as well," he reveals, "where I felt it was up to me to make their lives better or at least as problem-free as possible because, after all, that's what I'd been doing my whole life."

Nor did it end there. When he was on his own in the latter stages of his career, running a thriving one-person business, he felt as heavily accountable, not only to his business for its success or failure but also to his clients.

What a blessing, then, at the age of sixty-five and retired, no longer to be accountable in the same sense or to the extent that he had been his entire life, Carrington exults: "No boss, no clients, no company to manage. My parents are deceased. My children are adults and successfully on their way in the world. My former wife is also comfortably retired."

And so, with enormous relief, he finds the dead weight of responsibility lifted from his shoulders. He acknowledges his continuing obligations to society: to pay taxes, obey the law, be a proper neighbor, treat people well, love his family, and cherish his friends.

But it's a genuine pleasure, a tremendous joy, he says, to be alone and free at last of his burden of accountability.

Some of the new hermits are *downshifters*, a word coined by Amy Saltzman of *U.S. News & World Report* to describe a phenomenon that surfaced in the last decade: "the deliberate pursuit of greater personal fulfillment on a slower, more private professional track," in Saltzman's words.

Valerie Young calls it "The Great Work Debate: Money vs. Happiness." A former cubicle-dweller who publishes *Changing Course*, a newsletter for "people who want to live life on purpose, work at what they love, and follow their own road," she now helps others discover "creative alternatives to having a job."

Young credits the sudden death of her mother for shocking her into the realization that predictability is a double-edged sword—that if she didn't take control of her life, she was destined to remain "miserably well off," as she puts it.

Is the thought of earning less money scary? "You bet," says Young. "That's why I stayed in my own high-stress job as long as I did. Then, without warning, my mother died of a heart attack. She was five months away from retirement."

Walking away from a steady job with good benefits was risky, she concedes. "To me, though, the real risk is a headstone that reads: 'She wasn't happy, but she had a good dental plan.' For me, the debate is over."

Some new hermits are members of the "voluntary simplicity" movement: men and women grown weary of striving for material ends, of living for everyone but themselves, who are making do with less income and fewer material possessions in order to have more time for the important things.

Others are aging baby boomers, part of a cresting demographic wave that will lift the tide of Americans sixty-five and older to 77 million—20 percent of the U.S. population—by the year 2045. And though they arrive kicking and screaming, bristling with nervous energy, disavowing their "green old age," as Dryden called it, millions of boomers are navigating two of life's passages at once: middle age and parenthood.

Confronted with their mortality and the desire to pass along the right values to their children, quality-of-life choices have become paramount to them. And so, more and more boomers are looking inside themselves, inventing new ways to live and work, attempting to find a "path with heart," in Carlos Castañeda's words.

In their search for meaning in their lives, some have come to Richard Bode's defining realization: "I do not want to struggle anymore. I do not want to please. I do not seek the trappings of money, power, or success. I do not need a trophy on my wall or a corner office with a potted plant. I do not desire a house that others envy every time they drive by. All I want is a life of my own."

Dancing with Headhunters author G. J. Meyer puts it this way: "I have friends who wear gold Rolexes and cashmere sports coats, but when you get to know them it turns out that they regard their own lives as misbegotten messes of fear and greed and disappointment.... Their idea of fulfillment has come down to six days of golf a week."

But not even golf is about escaping the demands of career and family anymore. No longer a healthful respite from a stressful world in a bucolic setting, a way of being alone but not *too* alone, golf, along with everything else in our supersonic age, is about getting away *and* exercise *and* productivity, for this is the age of multitasking. The advertising exhortation, "Don't leave home without it!" now implies a beeper, cell phone, Palm Pilot, and laptop along with your trusty credit card—wherever you're headed.

Mark Twain called golf "a good walk spoiled," yet even the walking golfer is becoming an oxymoron, for leisurely traffic isn't good for business—on fairways or in shopping malls—so it won't be long before golf carts are mandatory on our nation's courses.

But it's not just about squandering the rare opportunities for pause and reflection in a world of ceaseless motion and activity; or that given these oases of calm, we compulsively glut and accelerate them. Most disturbing of all is that we've come to regard the anxiety and tension generated by an obsession with optimal efficiency and performance as desirable rather than destructive traits of modern living.

"I *can* have it all!" has become the rallying cry of a nation strung out on acquisitiveness and speed.

"Stress has become the badge of honor of the millennium," observes Manhattan psychologist Arlene Kagle in a *New York Times* article. "It's almost as if we're not allowed to enjoy what we're doing anymore, as if our lives are getting in the way of something that's more important. We lost the idea of the Sabbath as a day of rest long ago," Kagle adds.

"Now we have lost evenings, nights, and weekends as well. We're too busy banking online or buying clothes off the Internet. Then we complain—that is to say, brag—that we're just so wound up and tense we can barely sleep: four hours a night at most, and don't be getting me jealous by insisting that you get only three."

Chapter Two

Gone to Innisfree:
Journey to the Undiscovered Country

*Every once in a while I awaken
to the reality that I'm all I've got.*
—CLARK E. MOUSTAKAS

In January of 1994, I moved—I mean *really* moved. I, my old dog Britt, and an iguana named Mel. "Gone to the Beach," read the change-of-address notice I tucked into my greeting cards that Christmas: "I haven't retired, just retreated. This year I stopped the world and got off. On Washington's North Beach Peninsula, about a mile from Oysterville. Drop by for a beer if you're in the neighborhood. If I'm not home, check the beach. I'll probably be walking the dog."

Yes, indeed.

Surfside is a far smaller place than anywhere I'd lived before: minuscule, nondescript, inconsequential alongside Portland, Miami, New York, Chicago, San Francisco, and Hong Kong, my former cities of residence before this galactic leap of faith.

It's a reclusive place, the last knuckle on a rain-scoured finger of land lapped by the beige waters of Willapa Bay and the gray Pacific, wrapped by khaki sands and olive clouds, except in summer, when the sky is the color of washed denim. Here, wind and water lean on the land, thrusting a constant coolness from across the sea, buffing the stars at night to an awesome brilliance.

Yet, on the morning after my precipitous move, I wrote in my journal: "Took our first walk on the beach, me and Britt. Had a scared, hollow, desperate feeling inside me the whole time. I'm lonely today—for the crowded city and all the people I've purposely fled. I have to keep reminding myself why I did it, that nothing is forever. Paths ventured on can be reversed. God, I sound like Hamlet."

Another entry, later that first day: "It's an afternoon like the one when I first saw this house—cold and somber, a gloomy rain mottling the leaden surface of the canal below. But it seemed peaceful to me then, comforting and picturesque. Today it just seems grim. What if I'd rented that townhouse on the Willamette in downtown Portland instead of sinking everything into this godforsaken wedge of sand? How would I feel right now, watching the rain falling on the river in Portland? Probably worse because I'd have abandoned a dream. I know the changes I have to make aren't geographical, they're inside me. But can I bear to be alone long enough to make them?"

Anxiety, Kierkegaard affirms, is the dizziness of freedom.

Iguana Mel and faithful old Britt loved the beach right off. Most days of our first summer there together, Mel could be found gazing out a living room window, following the sun and dreaming, no doubt, of bright green love.

Britt, however, lasted only until the fall. She was a very old dog and a cherished friend who deserved her last bright season drowsing in sun-warmed sand, but I wished that she could have been with me for one more summer. Six days after she died, I drove to Portland and returned with an eight-week-old Australian Shepherd named Buddy Holly Fisher. That's the name I scrawled on the American Kennel Club papers I never mailed because I wound up spending the registration fee on a bottle of scotch to toast the rest of our lives together. I could do without people, I quickly found out, but not having a dog by my side would be intolerable.

And so we've lived these past six years—one writer, one lizard, and one pup—in a snug little house by a canal, a stroll away from the tawny sands of the blue Pacific. It's what I had dreamed of for a very long time.

The American Dream isn't fame or fortune—never was, never will be, not for most of us. It's taking control of our lives. The real dream is grounded in the primal satisfaction of succeeding on our own—independent, inner-directed, self-fulfilled, "life near the bone," as Henry David Thoreau put it.

The dream resonates with writers, painters, poets, and artists, in particular, for when they are alone they are closest to themselves, their creativity, and their reason for being. The same holds true for others preoccupied with finding a measure of coherent justification for what Elbert Hubbard, at the turn of the twentieth century, called "just one damn thing after another"—an accurate enough depiction of twenty-first-century life.

They are men and women who are asking themselves, in T. S. Eliot's words, "Where is the Life we have lost in living?"

They have heard Jean de la Bruyere's gloomy summation of man's existence: "He is not conscious of being born, he dies in pain, and he forgets to live."

And their wish for themselves is the same sentiment Jonathan Swift extended to a friend: "May you *live* all the days of your life."

They yearn, as did Thoreau, to fulfill their divine purpose "deliberately" and "as imagined." In growing numbers, they are heeding his practical advice: "The man who goes alone can start today; but he who travels with another must wait till that other is ready."

But what if their companions demur in the plaintive words of Emily Dickinson?

I cannot live with You—
It would be Life—
And Life is over there—
Behind the Shelf.

For these tentative Thoreaus, a time-share cottage at Walden Pond might be preferable to a primary residence, for though we covet a tranquil place in which to be still and serene, to touch once more our true and natural selves, we can bear these pastoral retreats only for so long.

Conditioned by society to regard those who choose to be alone with contempt tinged with awe, we think of new hermits as did Samuel Johnson: "The solitary mortal is certainly luxurious, probably superstitious, and possibly mad."

In our supersonic age fixated on unrelenting achievement, we look on them with a mixture of envy and suspicion, for as Thomas Merton noted,

"The solitary is necessarily a man who does what he wants to do. In fact, he has nothing else to do. That is why his vocation is both dangerous and despised. Dangerous because, in fact, he must become a saint by doing what he wants to do, instead of doing what he does not want to do. It is very hard to be a saint by doing what you like."

Women are much more ambivalent than men about being alone, says Ann Gallagher, fifty-three, a librarian, writer, wife, and mother of four adult children. An energetic, involved member of her community, Gallagher is one of those compassionate, giving people whose permanent withdrawal from the world would make it a poorer place. Yet she nurtures and protects her restorative periods of solitude, retreating alone to the family's coastal cottage whenever her active personal and professional life permits.

"Solitude is a huge, ambivalent topic for women," she remarks. "It's why so many books on this hypnotic subject have been written by us. Most women admire other women who venture off on their own, but they'd never do it themselves. Or even admit to a desire to do so. I say this from experience."

Her work, activities, and involvements are a joy, assures Gallagher, but only when they're balanced by her time away—time she prefers to spend entirely by herself. Many of her friends, she reveals, have expressed grudging admiration for her propensity for going off alone, while at the same time questioning, "Aren't you afraid?" "Don't you get lonely?"

"They remind me of the terrors that await The Woman Alone," she says, amusement creasing her pleasant features. "Violence. Rape. Blown fuses. Mechanical breakdowns on dark, rural roads."

Gallagher's grin spreads as she recites their litany of potential woes awaiting the woman alone: "Snow. Sleet. Floods. Other natural disasters. Power outages. Broken bones. No phone in case of any of the above. Worse, no phone at all. 'What do you *do* at the beach by yourself?' they ask, the question invariably posed with concern and furrowed brow. Eyes roll when I answer, 'I stare a lot.' 'At what?' they ask with nervous laughter. 'Into space,' I tell them truthfully. 'At the ocean. At the mountains. In between, I walk. And I stare some more.'"

"If instead I say, 'Oh, I write,' which is also true, although staring and walking always come first, my friends nod, relieved. 'Ah, yes, of course, she writes when she's alone.' And that makes it almost all right, not quite so crazy-seeming."

But reminders of The Terrors always follow, Gallagher says: "Darkness. Sleeping alone. Old door locks. Sounds of the fishermen's voices at 5:00 A.M. The slam of their pickup truck doors. No shades on the windows. The quiet. Nothing to do . . ."

We've lost sight of the individual, laments author Hal Borland: "Everything from singing to games, from travel to nature-watching has become a group activity. The person who wants to do anything alone, even just sit and think, has to fight off all the organizers."

As a child of twelve growing up in southern Oregon, Gallagher relates, she left her house one morning to walk into town. " 'You're going into town *alone?*' my mother asked me in consternation. When I said yes, she told me that if people saw me wandering by myself, they'd say, 'That girl must not have any friends.'"

"The words struck me like a brick: *That girl doesn't have any friends!*

"My mother's tone suggested this was a BAD thing to do: go around alone. Worse, a BAD thing to be: A girl without friends. We'd just moved into town," Gallagher continues, no longer smiling, "and the truth is there hadn't been enough time to make any friends, especially for a gawky preteen girl. Twelve is such a pivotal age for children, girls in particular, and for years afterwards I'd hear my mother's voice when I walked alone: *People will think you have no friends.*"

Gallagher gives a hearty laugh, but sadness lingers in her face. "At fifty-three," she says softly, "I'd say, *let* 'em! But for a girl of twelve . . ."

She doesn't finish the sentence, lost in her thoughts.

———————————

"We yearn for Walden Pond," cautions writer Ted Morgan, "and forget that one can drown in Walden Pond."

Or on the edge of an ocean, without ever setting foot in the water, as I feared I would when I moved to the beach.

It seems such a formidable feat, being alone, because society bludgeons into our collective consciousness that no man or woman is an island, that a solitary existence is cruel and unusual punishment meted out by a vengeful god for unpardonable sins.

Little wonder, then, that so many of us can only bear to be by ourselves when we're firmly connected to others, as if by a deep-sea diver's lifeline or in a sturdy shark cage, capable of being hoisted out of harm's way. Only when we're securely tethered, assured that we're fully protected and can quickly pull ourselves back up to safety, are we willing to descend into the murky depths of ourselves.

Overheard in cyberspace:

"I'm thirty-one years old and single, living in what I feel is a married world. I sometimes wonder how people who stay single forever find value in their lives. I'm not saying they're not valuable, but everyone around me is concerned with their kids' events, be they sports, band, theater, it doesn't matter. 'Will Jimmy get the lead in the play?' 'Will Bobby make the football team?' Or it's their spouse. Their whole life is built around their family.

"This is fine. It's what our culture encourages. And it's why I fight with myself often. If I'm not married, there's no one out there who finds me worthy enough to spend the rest of their life with, then ... I don't know. I think about this a lot.

"I think I'm valuable. I have an important job where I'm liked and wanted. But many times it's not enough for me. When that weekend rolls around—or any night for that matter—and I want to do something, friends go with me if their family is 'OK' with it. Or if the family isn't busy with other things. Yes, yes, they make time for me....

"My point is, they want to spend time with their family. That's who they want to be with on holidays. That's who they want to share good news (or bad) with first. That's who they get excited about seeing. If I never have a family and view these things as 'priorities,' then I'll never be high on someone's 'priority list.'

"I'll not be a mother, wife, daughter-in-law, etc., therefore, what is my importance? I know I have to find it within myself, but it's not that simple. And I wish I was one of those people who says, 'I have God in my life, therefore I'm not lonely.' Well, God doesn't play scrabble with me. He doesn't sit with me at the movies, and he's not there to hug me, literally, when I'm feeling I need one.

"Yes, I believe in God. I pray. I talk with him often. But I'm not one of those who is not lonely because God is in my life. I wish it was that easy for me. I guess it's just loneliness. If people knew, they'd be surprised I feel this way.

"I have loads of friends. I teach elementary school and am the most loved teacher at my school. Yet, there is an emptiness. As I get older, I try to come to terms with this. I think this may be my lot. Maybe marriage isn't in my future. I don't know how I'll handle it. I try to prepare myself. Sometimes I'm OK with it. Other times, no, and it's overwhelming."

And so I rose and went to my Innisfree. To a snug little house, not of wattles and clay in a bee-loud glade as in Yeats's poem, but where the murmur of sea on sand lulls my gimcrack spirit.

Here, I've become like Anne Morrow Lindbergh's open, empty beach, "erased by today's tides of all of yesterday's scribblings."

But not the memories.

They came flooding back first, coursing over the weirs of denial I'd built to hold them at bay, for as long as I can remember.

With the memories came the remorse, the renounced sorrow of a lifetime of failed choices, lost opportunities—all the irretrievable acts of love and courage and kindness that had never been consummated because I hadn't understood their importance until it was too late.

I was one of those people who had always sought himself in others, shunning my own company as if it were diseased, cramming my life with activities and people in search of the person I wanted to be, yet never searching in myself, always in others.

But the time came when I desperately needed to narrow my quest, to return, in Doris Grumbach's words, to "the core of myself, to discover what was in there, no matter how deeply hidden." To see if the things I could give myself were better than what I'd sought from others, to put my life on an even keel and keep it there, to wake up each morning with the day the same as I'd left it the night before.

There were no answers in those first anxious months at the beach, only fearful questions. How long could I endure this cold, gray place before it seeped into my soul and destroyed me? Could I bear the regrets I'd repressed for so long? How could I survive my loneliness alone when I could hardly bear it in the midst of others? What dreams would find me when I could no longer flee them?

And if I ran now, again, would I be running forever, with all hope abandoned of finding—what? What was I looking for anyway?

Coming to the beach meant facing my deepest disquiets, my despairing unease with who I really was and all I would never become. It meant confronting all the curdled remorse, the disavowed guilt that seems to struggle to the surface when everything else is still.

It meant discovering if I could be complete alone, not merely as an adjunct of someone else, whether I needed others to energize and validate myself, to make me feel of some worth and consequence.

It meant asking myself questions I'd never dared raise. It meant learning if I could stand the answers.

I had desperately sought my salvation in others. With time getting short, could I find it in myself? "Nine-tenths of wisdom," someone once wrote, "is being wise in time." If I let this time for reckoning pass, would it ever come again?

Chapter Three

It's About Time:
The Only Real Wealth

I would willingly stand at
street corners, hat in hand,
begging passersby to drop
their unused minutes into it.
—BERNARD BERENSON

Winter again. The summer people have gone. The early morning walks are solitary once more. Fog wraps the ocean and sky like a wet gray glove. Sprinting through the frosty dune grass, my dog Buddy emerges soaked and grinning. He's become a man-child, his boundless puppy love and mindless exuberance caroming off the walls in a muscular body. He lives by one rule: To be alive is to be gloriously happy. Not a bad way to be, I often remind myself.

Comfortable in the ebb and flow of each other's idiosyncracies and needs, he keeps me company while I work, I join him often in his play. His unflagging high spirits urge me to cram activity and joy into every waking moment as he does. By so doing, I tell myself, I will multiply my allotted time by dog years and dilate the remaining seasons accordingly. A good way to look at life, I figure.

I'd have liked to exchange high fives with a nationally syndicated newspaper columnist after reading her reply to a fifty-six-year-old woman who wrote that she was engaged to "a wonderful man who was perfect in every way—except one. He hated dogs." And she had a German Shepherd that she loved dearly.

Her fiancé would not allow her to keep the animal after they were married, the worried woman said, adding, "I love this man and want to spend the rest of my life with him, but I'm not sure how much it would hurt me to give up my pet."

Alas, what should she do?

"If you want to enjoy life, keep the dog and give up your fiancé," the columnist replied. "Any man who would demand that you give up your beloved pet is no bargain and doesn't know the meaning of love."

Alone at the beach, the epiphanies have come fast and furious, partly because I've had so much time to think, partly because I've been searching for the answers for so long. But I'm starting to "get it" at last. Everything seems simpler now, incredibly clear. I think solitude does that: it rewards you for taking the time and summoning the courage to face yourself—something you must do alone.

One thing I know for sure, it's not about soul, as Billy Joel sings, it's about time. Time, I've come to realize, is the most precious possession I own: vast, uncluttered, open-ended, with a core of deep white silence like the storms that shroud this winter shore.

Luxurious time to spend wantonly without the need to count its passing. Time devoted to nothing, if that is what I choose, time to lavish on the things meaningful only to me.

Time to think. Or not think, just feel, just *be*.

Time to stare, like Ann Gallagher, at the stillness within.

Time to remember, to grieve, to mourn—something I'd never done.

Time to ask for forgiveness. Time to forgive, myself most of all.

Time to examine my life and the people in it who have mattered to me, and I to them. Time to say, "I love you."

Time to see myself plainly, and all the things that made me who I am.

Time to change what I can, to make peace with what I can't, to wipe the slate clean by a cleansing sea.

But gaining this wealth of time meant relinquishing all of the people and places and things I'd clung to for so long to make time pass quickly, to avoid feeling alone.

The good news was I now had all of this time I had spent on meaningless distractions. The bad news was I had all of this time, without the meaningless distractions.

———————

Ask virtually anyone these days, "How are things going?" "How's work?" "How's life?"

The inevitable answer: "Busy!" The word is blurted instinctively, as if it were simply the most acceptable response.

The measure of our worth seems to lie in the total expenditure of our time. In a world with no time, busyness has become the red badge of courage and fulfillment, a noble end rather than a necessary means.

"A sign of a good executive," a movie mogul was quoted in *Los Angeles* magazine, "is someone who doesn't return phone calls." What he meant, I guess, is that if you have time left over to answer phone calls, you're not busy enough making deals.

"It's worse than dog eat dog," laments Woody Allen's character in his 1989 movie, *Crimes and Misdemeanors*. "It's dog doesn't return other dogs' phone calls, which is terrible."

So many people simply don't respond anymore, particularly in business and professional matters. The unspoken attitude is, "What part of my not getting back to you didn't you understand?"

What's more, we've conditioned ourselves *not* to expect an answer, buying right into the premise that people who don't respond literally don't have a moment to spare. In an age of instant communications, but a world with no time except for those who can show us the money, the nonreply has become a legitimate response. We've actually come to expect it as standard protocol, from just about anyone from whom we need something but who doesn't need anything from us.

And that's too bad, because it's not about being turned down, it's about being ignored. To older folks, in particular—to a generation that continues to regard deliberate tardiness and the failure to communicate as inexcusable bad manners—people who don't respond are particularly abrasive.

It's true, the demise of good manners shouldn't concern solitaires striving to extricate themselves from the slights of all those necessarily aloof individuals. Leave them to heaven, their self-importance, and the corporate shareholders. Nonetheless, I've become inordinately grateful for civility, another victim of our harried times.

"We skitter about like hyperactive gerbils," observes Amy Krouse Rosenthal, "high not just on caffeine, but on caffeine's luscious byproduct, productivity. Ah, the joy of doing, accomplishing, crossing off."

And, oh yes, making money. The trouble is, even if our need for money diminishes, our compulsion to keep busy doesn't. Busyness, however mindless and unnecessary, becomes essential to our sense of relevance and well-being. It's a way, says Rosenthal, of intimating, "My time is filled, my phone doesn't stop ringing, and you, therefore, should think well of me."

Americans, after all, are miles ahead of everyone else in mining the economic value of time, points out John E. Johnson. But lost in the process, says the noted teacher of pastoral theology, are our bearings, our sense of proportion, the timeless cadence of life set by "the cycles and the seasons, in the rising and setting of the sun, the phases of the moon, high tide and low tide, snow fall and runoff."

Instead of using all your available time to play catch-up, do some reflecting, urges Johnson: "Remember who you really are, and realize afresh what is really important. Take stock of the time left before the kids will be on their own. Restore eternity to the soul, get in sync with what is real. Only by seeing where we have been can we hope to have a clue to where we need to be going. And then life may just not be so loony—so banal and profane, reduced to punching keys. Life will once again be anchored down."

Joan Roth, thirty-eight, gave herself the gift of time in the form of an eighteen-month hiatus from men. Blonde, strikingly pretty, highly personable, she had never lacked for suitors. But after the breakup of a six-year relationship that followed an eleven-year marriage, Roth decided she needed some time to see what she really wanted, to develop her sense of self so that if she decided to have another relationship, she would do it from a place of strength, not neediness.

"One of the happiest, freest times of my life was that year and a half I spent alone," reveals Roth.

"I lived by myself for the first time ever and loved every minute of it! I refused to date, took my first vacation alone, and really came to appreciate my own company. In retrospect, it was the best thing I possibly could have done for myself."

Apparently so, for she married again six months ago. But had she not taken those eighteen months off, says Roth, she may not have found the exactly right person to partner with, even though the most difficult adjustment she's had to make has been relinquishing the alonetime she came to cherish.

"My husband is very sweet," Roth says. "He has a gentle spirit and honors my independence. He's probably the only person I could live with after having been alone. My new stepson, on the other hand, presents a current challenge. He's an eleven-year-old boy with whom I'm going through a difficult adjustment period."

So, togetherness for her right now—after a year and a half of blissful aloneness—is a "six-of-one/half-a-dozen-of-the-other kind of thing," she adds wistfully.

"A bit of advice I gladly pass along to the 'Oh, my God, I'm alone—I need to run out and find another man!' crowd is: 'Don't do it! Take a break. Give yourself the time off we all need between relationships.'

"Don't be so afraid of being alone that you rush right back into something for which you'll soon be sorry. Had I not forced myself to wait a while, had I not taken the time to be alone, to figure out what I really wanted, I might not have been ready to meet the person I finally married."

Screen star Melanie Griffith said pretty much the same thing in a *PARADE* magazine article by Ellen Hawkes. In the summer of 1994, reports Hawkes, Griffith and her third husband, Don Johnson, separated. Griffith then spent a few months alone, "doing a lot of soul-searching." That period was very significant for her, said the actress, explaining:

"Before, nobody had wanted me to take my life in my own hands. I felt I finally had to find my own identity and what really mattered to me. I didn't want to be defined by others' expectations anymore."

The following February, Griffith met Spanish actor Antonio Banderas. As the world knows, they married in 1996 and had a daughter that September. Today, at forty-two, after three divorces, single motherhood, a stint in rehab, and a great deal of soul-searching, she wears her heart—not on her sleeve but tattooed on her right shoulder, with her husband's first name etched in the center: Antonio.

"I think that time of self-reflection during the summer prepared me for meeting Antonio," Griffith told Hawkes. "I needed to be strong in myself before I could fall in love and feel safe. That's what I'm going to teach my daughters—that they have to value themselves first before they jump into love or define themselves by men."

For most of her life, says Joanne Douglas, she expected someone to hand her a magical block of time.

"I always thought this time would come when all my obligations were taken care of," says Douglas, sixty-six. "But I know now that no one is just going to hand it to me, that if I really want the time to do the things that are important to me, I'm going to have to *take* it."

"Give *yourself* the gift of time," she exhorts.

"I've never quite learned how to do that. There was always family to take care of. It was an obligation when the children were small. But now that they're grown and self-sufficient, they can be put on 'hold,' even though they're still important parts of my life. So finally I can put some of my needs before theirs. But why is that so difficult to do without a guilt trip?

"Is it because my life as a mother consisted of so much giving that I don't know how to do anything else? Is it my makeup because my astrological sign is Cancer? Is it the 'good girl' syndrome most of us are raised with? I didn't have the guilt of a Roman Catholic upbringing, but we Anglicans do a pretty good job with that, too.

"My grandmother believed strongly in reincarnation, but I've decided to hedge my bets and do everything I want the first time around because I may not get a second chance. So I ask myself, 'What do I want to accomplish this first and probably *only* time around?'

"Well, for a few years now, I've been dabbling in genealogy. I have a fascinating great-great-grandfather, great-grandfather, and his father-in-law, all of whom I feel should have a book or booklet or at least a chapter written about them. I have notebooks of material on them, and I need to begin writing. I must give myself the time to do this. It won't materialize on its own. Trouble is, if it did, I'd probably use the time to take a nap.

> "My grandmother believed strongly in reincarnation, but I've decided to hedge my bets and do everything I want the first time around because I may not get a second chance. So I ask myself, 'What do I want to accomplish this first and probably only time around?'"

"But I've begun to give myself the gift of one day a week, more or less. Where am I finding this time? I'm taking it away from the not-so-important things in my life and transferring that precious time to those parts of my life where I'm completely alone in making decisions and initiating actions that affect me—all the things that are important to *me*."

In the golden autumn of 1996, Buddy and I embarked on a six-week, sixteen-state journey of 15,000 miles in search of new hermits. It was something I suddenly wanted to do, and when I couldn't think of a single reason not to, I set out. Not long on the open road, though, a sense of eerie displacement came over me, as if I were the only person left on earth with enough time to drive casually across the country, the last easy rider in a transonic land.

William Least Heat Moon's "blue highways," I quickly discovered, had faded into Americana, displaced by freeways of frantic pursuit. Even George and Martha behind the wheel of their retirement Winnebago are in a hurry.

This uncanny feeling may have been triggered by a postcard I received from author Kathleen Norris the day before I embarked on my travels with Buddy. Several weeks earlier I'd written to her, requesting a meeting of whatever duration she could afford, in the hope of securing a few quotes for this book. My travels would take me past her rural Midwest town, I explained, and whatever time she could spare would be greatly appreciated.

"Sorry," she demurred in her postcard, "but my schedule won't permit an interview." It was the word "schedule" that lingered with me as I set forth on my quest for new hermits, for it frayed the cherished image of this eloquent author cloaked in contemplative stillness beside her beloved monks.

Upon forsaking Manhattan to move back to the Great Plains of her youth, Mrs. Norris found the land's silent call "powerful without being seductive," leading her not "aside or astray, but home," as she recorded in her enthralling book, *Dakota: A Spiritual Geography*.

Perhaps, too, the word stayed with me because a few days earlier I'd come across an illustration in *Utne Reader* of a tonsured monk on the run, briefcase in hand, newspaper under an arm, breathlessly hailing a cab. "Monks in Overdrive," read the title of the accompanying article, excerpted from the *National Catholic Reporter*, which made the case that work, American style, is destroying monastic life as we romantically picture it.

There's nothing particularly monastic about monastic life these days, Gregory J. Millman pointed out in his iconoclastic piece, quoting Father Timothy Joyce of Glastonbury Abbey in Massachusetts: "Monastics have become workaholics, always rushing around. I don't think our life is any different from anyone else's."

What a dismal thought. And how different from the gentle image evoked by *Dakota*'s closing words: "Soon, the monks, too, will begin to sing, the gentle lullaby of vespers and compline, at one with the rhythm of evening, the failing light and the rise of the moon. Together, monks and coyotes will sing the world to sleep."

In sharp contrast, Millman's article concluded with a discouraging remark by Father Terrence Kardong of Kathleen Norris's own adoptive monastery, Assumption Abbey in Richardton, North Dakota: "You have an option of being shaped by culture or trying to follow your calling. Our calling is not to be tossed around by the storms of culture. We can decide our lifestyle. But how poor do you want to be?"

Ah, there's the rub. How poor do you want to be?

"As poor as it takes," I wish Father Kardong had added, but he didn't.

Someone, after all, has to keep the wolf from the door, even from monastery porticoes. And if even monastics are overworked and harried, unable to keep themselves from being sucked into the money trap, what hope is there for the rest of us?

After passing, then, through Bozeman and Billings, I plunged into the prairie vastness of Wyoming, and then the amber emptiness of South Dakota where it parallels Nebraska. "The sky is a dome of eggshell blue tapering to turquoise at its edges, the land an ocean of hills and hollows," I wrote in my journal that glorious afternoon.

The whole month of October turned out to be magical, each Indian Summer day as benign as the one before it. Driving through Minnesota's saffron fields stretching to the edges of the sky, I wondered if what Kathleen Norris might have told me would have been as worthwhile as the things I had found for myself.

But I already knew the answer.

Nearing Madison, Wisconsin, where my daughter was entering the final weary months of her doctoral pursuit, I paused to watch a cooling wind stroke a hillside trembling with the russet leaves of fall and learned the meaning of "quaking aspen."

We talked for the first time in her Santa Fe apartment, as tiny as the 9' × 12' cabin in which she had spent most of her eight years alone in the north Idaho woods.

At the age of thirty-two, Susan Baumgartner had lived as a hermit in a simple frame structure without a bathroom, electricity, or running water, in a remote canyon on the breaks of the Potlatch River, east of Genesee where she was born. Without a job or a car, though, she ran out of money after a year and had to interrupt her solitary lifestyle in the Idaho wilderness.

The University of Idaho graduate who had previously scrubbed toilets at an Oregon resort, packed fish at an Alaska cannery, and clerked at a morgue in Connecticut, decided to head east for a master's degree in literature from Syracuse University, then stayed in Syracuse to launch a career in technical writing while she collected rejection slips for the seven novels she had written to date.

But four years later, Baumgartner was back at her tiny Idaho cabin—with a car for the necessary commute to a part-time job teaching freshman English at the University of Idaho. And this time she stayed for seven years, teaching three days a week with summers off, which allowed her to sleep at the cabin five days of the week during the school year, and spend the whole time there in the summer.

So Baumgartner again chopped wood and hauled water from a nearby spring. At night she lit candles and propane lamps, their comforting light supplemented by a single bulb powered by a small solar panel. She cooked her meals on a propane stove, heated the cabin with firewood, used a blue plastic dishpan as a sink, kept an ice chest on the north side of the cabin as a refrigerator, and traipsed to a nearby outhouse.

And she wrote a book she called *My Walden: Tales from Dead Cow Gulch*, in which she made this telling observation: "Everyone knows how 'to do.' But most of us experience 'to be' so rarely, we don't know how to be when we finally get there. 'To be or not to be?' Hamlet knew the agony well and expressed it perfectly."

"The whirl of our world comes to a stop, and we panic, realizing that suddenly we have time to look at ourselves, to look at our lives, to experience introspection. So we quickly turn on the television or hurry out to go shopping, lest we be forced to see what we have become.

"It's a lot of work just to be. You must overcome guilt and years of conditioning. You must face emotions like sadness and disappointment and confusion and despair. You must suddenly become accountable for your life. Instead of mindlessly letting life slip through your fingers, you must grab hold and husband the time you have and make it mean something."

And she ends her book with these affirming words: "Winter is good. I've learned to survive it well, to experience its quiet joys, but the seasons coming up—spring, summer, fall—melt, growth, harvest—these are the months I live for. That is what I love. I go back into the cabin and close the door. . . . My mind fills with possibilities. Time to begin another year of life here on Dead Cow Gulch."

But when I caught up with her in October 1996, Baumgartner's journey to herself had taken her to New Mexico. "Most of the years at Dead Cow Gulch were good, except for that last bittersweet year when I decided to leave," she told me in her minuscule one-room apartment in Santa Fe—"luxurious" nonetheless to the hermit of Genesee, now forty-seven years old.

"I started seeing clearly how much time I spent simply surviving, chopping wood and carrying water. I wondered if I was losing a precious part of life in just struggling to survive," she said wistfully.

"And yet, a less intense experience might not have gotten me as far as it did. It was like an unending Outward Bound experience, constantly pushing my boundaries. Without the difficulty and challenge, the highs wouldn't have been there."

Baumgartner gave an example: "A couple of times a year, I had to climb on the roof to the skylight to clear it of debris. It was always terrifying. 'I'll fall,' I'd tell myself. 'I'll lie here in pain for days, then die.' And each time, it was a huge triumph. 'I'm stronger, braver now than I was before,' I'd tell myself afterwards."

The plan at first was *no* plan, she said.

"I'd always had an intense need for solitude. When I began writing in 1973, I assumed I'd always be writing—alone. To me, other work has always been a waste of time. The ultimate dream was solitude without the need to work. The cabin allowed me to work less and write more, which has always been one of my primary goals.

"I was extremely productive there as a writer, partly because there were no interruptions or distractions, and partly because, over time, the cabin became drenched with the habit of productivity."

Not only were her published book and seven completed novels evidence of this motivation and energy, but the essays, articles, and op-ed pieces she began selling to a variety of regional magazines and newspapers were proof as well. "Like Pavlov's dog, even as I walked toward the cabin after a day of teaching, the ideas would begin to gather in my head because I knew I could soon vent them safely into the computer. In the 'real' world, I was often compelled to repress them lest they make me crazy—all those thoughts circulating endlessly in my head with no focused time to get them down. I also stayed because I simply loved it," Baumgartner added.

"Part of it was the roots I was sinking. The longer I was at the cabin, the more precious everything there became. Sightings of the first buttercups each spring were amplified by the sightings of the seasons before.

"Each tree, every rock formation was steeped in memories. And those memories were intensified, in turn, because I had time to renew, embellish, and strengthen them by consciously experiencing what was around me.

"This intense consciousness is a luxury not always available to people who don't live alone, and particularly those in populated areas. They don't have time to fall in love with the life around them. Because they haven't been fortunate enough to be humbled through a long, intense association with nature, they may always be outsiders to their own ecosystem, unaware they are just a small, though integral part of the vast web of life around them.

"It's a kind of belonging not many people get to experience, and it's quite addictive and satisfying."

Baumgartner fell silent. I was about to ask her another question, thinking she'd moved on, when suddenly she spoke again:

"I want to be conscious. I want to notice that I'm alive while I'm living. I want to suck up every drop. It's mindfulness I treasure most. I realized early on that I have a slow brain. I can't do multitasking. The world moves too quickly for me. When I get caught up in it, I lose all awareness of my own existence. Consequently, I've always tried to find ways to slow down, to live apart, to protect that vulnerable part of me where my real life occurs. It's the same impulse, I think, of mystics, monks, transcendentalists, and academics. For us, spiritual and mental life is far more real than the physical. Whole worlds can rise and fall while I sit at my desk gazing out the window.

> "It's not solitude itself we hermits love, but what solitude gives us. Solitude is a means to an end, not an end in itself. It brings us things nobody else can give us."

"It's not solitude itself we hermits love, but what solitude gives us. Solitude is a means to an end, not an end in itself. It brings us things nobody else can give us. So perhaps I also stayed out of fear. The cabin came to be like a magical place to me, and the longer I stayed there, the more it became invested with magic. I began to doubt I could write anywhere else or stay plugged to that wonderful connected feeling with myself and all the life around me."

But the loneliness never went away completely, she revealed.

"From the cabin, I'd walk up a bluff occasionally and look at the lights of Moscow, Idaho, in the distance. With another dark night falling, I desperately wanted to be among those people, to walk with them, see a movie, enter a grocery store.

"The times of needing human contact would always be there, I realized, and all I could do was accept and manage that realization and that need and get by it."

She came to realize as well, Baumgartner said, that living alone brings a real stigma:

"Three or even four years ago, I was absolutely solid in my belief that solitude provided the only viable form of life for me. I still treasure what I learned from being totally alone, and I may very well go back to it. But I'm currently undergoing a test of my hermit faith.

"Having moved from the cabin and dramatically disrupted my life by coming to Santa Fe, I'm obviously in a questioning period again—once again reexamining the whole premise on which I've built my life.

"I ask myself, 'Could I learn to function in the real world without losing the parts of myself that feel most precious?' 'Can I justify slighting the sexual and social aspects of my life in order to nourish my spirituality?' 'Does the spiritual realm even exist, or is it merely an excuse to avoid the issues I really need to deal with?'

"Even when hermits experience great mystic joy in their solitude, the loud clamor of everyone else can still shake their confidence. I'd like to believe this isn't so, but I'm afraid it is. We peer out at the rest of the world from our cabin windows and can't help wondering if we're missing something.

"It could just be the grass-is-always-greener syndrome, but I think to myself married people must feel the same way when they view the freedom of single people. And we singles can't help envying the intimacy of those who are married.

"Maybe solitude isn't *the* answer, I tell myself, but only one of the answers. Still, it's a luxury every individual should have the chance to experience because it's infinitely enriching. It's an adventure of the soul. No matter what the future holds for me, I'll always treasure my eight years at Dead Cow Gulch, as well as all the other periods of time I've devoted to solitude.

"What I've gained alone greatly exceeds anything I may have missed. I wouldn't give up those years for anything. But it's hard to hide from yourself when you're alone.

"Solitude makes you obsessively self-reflective, which is both a curse and a blessing, an affliction and a cure, all in one."

At the cabin, at each year's end, she would culminate her passionate ritual of writing in a daily journal. And every December 31, she would read the entire year's entries in one sitting.

"I did it," she explained, "as an examination of conscience, to visit and revisit the dark places that kept appearing, to be completely honest with myself so I could see and understand who I was and what I was doing and why."

Baumgartner then told about her long struggle to reconcile her discomfort as a straight woman, her conflict over not wanting to be with a man. "Removing myself was my way to deal with the dilemma of my sexuality," she said.

"It was a time to decide whether I would spend most of my life alone or be brave enough to find a way to be with others, both as a friend and a lover. It was part of the searching I've always done, the questioning of my need for aloneness, whether it was healthy or pathological, whether it sprung from love or fear." Baumgartner came out as a lesbian in 1991, two years after her return to Dead Cow Gulch.

She thinks she will find the answers in Santa Fe, she told me. "People come to Santa Fe for answers." Here, she'll decide which one of three courses is right for her.

"The first: 'Of course, I'm going back to the cabin. It's where I belong. This is where I was meant to be. Alone.' The second: 'I can do it *here*—and have electricity. And cultural enrichment. And other people.' The third: 'I don't miss the cabin. Nor is Santa Fe the answer. What do I try next?'"

She's open to the third option for the first time in her life, Baumgartner said, because something else happened that final year at Dead Cow Gulch.

"Initially," she revealed, "I felt I had to be in *that* place—where I was centered, where everything flowed through me, where I knew what was important and what wasn't and what I had to do. Then I came to realize I didn't need a particular place any longer, that it was all *inside* me now, that I could reach wherever I had to be through a psychological rather than a physical journey."

This is where I left Susan Baumgartner, contemplating the three forks in the long road on her journey to herself. It

> *"Maybe solitude isn't the answer, I tell myself, but only one of the answers. Still, it's a luxury every individual should have the chance to experience because it's infinitely enriching. It's an adventure of the soul."*

would be four years before I learned how far one of those junctures—and a man named Sean Gardner—had taken her.

Maybe it was the incongruous place we met that stirred my doubts about thirty-six-year-old Anne Wylie's pricey mode of self-discovery. Several days before her departure on a month-long religious retreat in Tibet, we chatted as she exercised in the weight room of her health club. The thrice-a-week regimen, she claimed, diffused her daily accumulation of vocational stress, and would I mind interviewing while she worked out? Not at all, I replied.

And so, between vigorous sets of arm curls, leg lifts, power squats, pull-downs, and bench presses, the toned and buffed intensive-care nurse talked about searching for herself in faraway places of silence and contemplation. Counting airfare, expenses, and an $800 contribution to the Buddhist monastery she would soon be visiting, Wylie figured that the forthcoming spiritual excursion would wind up costing her close to $3,000.

"You could buy yourself a luxury cruise or see half of Europe with that kind of money," I joshed. "Why spend it on a monastery room with no view?"

"To be physically near people pursuing their spirituality," she replied. "It's something that's become extremely important for me to do, a path I've been following for a long time."

Still, the image of her as a passive captive in the cloistered antiquity of a remote monastery seemed inconsistent with the energetic, gregarious dynamo pumping iron in front of me. Sensing my skepticism, Wylie went on gently. "I'm aware we all have to participate fully in the world around us. There are realities of modern life that are inflexible and permanent—the need to work, pay bills, survive economically—but everything else is in flux, constantly changing, forever different, even though we maintain mental constraints to deny the transience and perpetual newness around us. We all want to be happy, to find lasting love, meaning, purpose, and inner peace," she went on.

> "We each have within ourselves what we need for our own journey. The answers aren't out there, out in the world, but within us. And we will only hear those answers if we are quiet enough."

"But the mundane world can't give us these things because, by their nature, they're short-lived and fleeting despite our desperate efforts to preserve whatever brief semblance of them comes along. The only thing we can control is what we think, what we know, what we believe. The only permanence we can achieve is the knowledge of *ourselves*—the certainty of who we are and the person we need to be in order to be at peace with ourselves. And the only way to get there is by opening our minds and hearts to the love and creation that's constantly evolving around us, instead of living fearfully in the tiny prisons of our own realities."

Wylie grinned suddenly.

"*That's* why I go on long retreats instead of Club Med cruises. Now how about spotting me on my bench presses?"

My final stop on my autumn travels with Buddy before wheeling westward toward Phoenix, Reno, San Francisco, Portland, then southwest Washington and home, was a Jesuit retreat house on a tiny Wisconsin peninsula jutting into Lake Winnebago. Here, at a breathtaking place called Fahrnwold—once a millionaire's mansion, then a school for handicapped children, then a novitiate, and now a sanctuary of silence—I met with Father Richard McCaslin and Sister Marie Schwan.

At a picnic table wrapped by ancient oaks and an oyster-blue shoreline, I asked the two retreat directors, "Why do people come here? What are they seeking that they can't find elsewhere?" Neither answered for a few moments, then Father McCaslin spoke first.

"More," he said. "They're looking for *more*. They come in search of meaning, for purpose, to make contact with something else, something transcendent. They come to find peace, to find freedom, to satisfy a hunger deep inside them for more than what their daily lives have to offer. They come to fulfill the longings of their human heart. They come with the need to step inside themselves so they can step outside again in a more fulfilling way," the Jesuit priest added softly.

"They come to be quiet, to validate what they already know, to trust the authenticity of their own being. They know how to pray but they need the assurance they still can."

Father McCaslin lapsed into silence, and then Sister Marie spoke: "We help them track their own inner path, to follow God's footprints which are already there."

"We each have within ourselves what we need for our own journey. The answers aren't out there, out in the world, but within us. And we will only hear those answers if we are quiet enough."

"I see women on their journey, working so hard," Sister Marie said. "I have an image of their souls, stretched so tight they're pulling apart, strained taut, frayed at the edges. 'I invite you,' I tell them, 'to let your soul rest. Drop down into your deepest self and just rest, like a child in the arms of a good mother.'"

I drove away from Fahrnwold with that vibrant thought. And another:

We need to tell *ourselves* what we long to hear. For it will be truer than anything anyone else can tell us.

Chapter Four

Through Loss, Sorrow, Denial:
The Long Passage Home

Know thyself? If I knew
myself, I'd run away.
—GOETHE

Q: What is denial?

A: It's a river in Egypt.

A joke as old as the Nile—as old as denial itself.

But what is denial, in its dysfunctional sense, that is? We hear and read the word so much these days, I've often wondered exactly what it means.

The *Columbia Encyclopedia* defines denial as "an ego defense mechanism that operates unconsciously to resolve emotional conflict and allay anxiety by refusing to perceive the more unpleasant aspects of external reality," differentiating between "adaptive" denial, as happens in the first stage of coming to terms with death, and "maladaptive," or delusional denial.

It's beholding the mote in your brother's eye, says the Bible, while disregarding the beam in your own.

"Vanishing cream for the mind," English writer Jeremiah Creedon calls it.

Denial is refusing to listen to the voice that awakens you in the night and whispers, "You know, you really are an incredible jerk and you ought to do something about it!"

"Beware thoughts that come in the night," cautions William Least Heat Moon at the start of *Blue Highways*, his evocative journal of self-discovery on the back roads of America. "They aren't turned properly. They come in askew, free of sense and restriction, deriving from the most remote of sources."

Samuel Taylor Coleridge called those remote sources "an aching hollowness in the bosom, a dark cold speck at the heart, an obscure and boding sense of something that must be kept out of sight of the conscience; some secret lodger, whom they can neither resolve to reject or retain."

Denial is keeping from ourselves secrets we already know. It's choosing to forget what we can't bear to remember. It's making people tell us what we want to hear so that we can keep believing the lies we've told ourselves, keep punishing those who dare to make us listen to the truth.

Psychology Today senior editor Daniel Goleman gives it another name: lacuna, a psychological blind spot, a hole in our attention, a gap in our self-awareness.

> *Denial is keeping from ourselves secrets we already know. It's choosing to forget what we can't bear to remember.*

Denial is the psychology of self-deception, the mind's deliberate failure to see things as they really are in order to protect ourselves from ourselves, says the Harvard Ph.D. and author of *Vital Lies, Simple Truths: The Psychology of Self-Deception*.

Familiar words of denial:

"I am not a crook."

"I was only obeying orders."

"Business is business."

"It's not about the money."

"I can quit whenever I want."

"I don't remember."

The boy was twelve when he watched his father die, sixteen when he wrote an article that ran in his high school newspaper in April of 1950, under the notation, "This is a true story, written on the fourth anniversary of his father's death and dedicated to the memory of a great person by his son." It is what the boy remembered of what had happened in a suburb of Manila on the night of September 17, 1946:

THE FATHER

The big white house stood majestically on the street corner. Past a steel garden gate stood four huge pine trees, their green tops swaying softly in the evening breeze, their roots lost in a sea of neatly cropped grass.

It was evening now and the house was quiet under the rising moon. Occasionally, laughter could be heard from inside.

In the house lived one family. The father had just returned from his work at the office and was seated in the spacious living room, smoking and enjoying his glass of beer. His attention was focused on the evening paper. Seated around him was his family—four boys and a girl. His wife was at his side, happy just to be with him.

They were a handsome couple, both in their early forties. The man was fairly tall with piercing hazel eyes that twinkled now and again. His face revealed the kindness of his soul.

His wife was a slim woman, kind and patient. She still retained some of the beauty of her younger years.

After the children went to bed, they talked for a while, then ascended the stairs as well. Stillness soon enveloped the household, ending another evening similar to other evenings enjoyed by that family. Here was a family at peace with God and with the world.

It had been a quiet night. Three hours had elapsed since the couple had retired. The whole neighborhood was now asleep.

In the dim shadow of the house slunk five men. They circled it once, then came upon a window that looked like the easiest illicit entrance. They forced open the window with a coiled wire, then quietly dropped inside.

Here, the leader in hushed tones ordered two to remain and stay on guard. Leaving the two behind, the trio passed the living room and entered the kitchen. They stumbled on the sleeping houseboy.

Quickly, one prodded him awake. "Show us your master's bedroom," he ordered fiercely.

The quavering manservant led them to the door of his master's bedroom.

They wrenched open the door and burst in. Nimbly one scrambled to the bedside and quickly relieved the master of the gun he was reaching for under his pillow. He stuck the .45-caliber gun in his waistband and turned on the lights. All of them were barefooted and all had handkerchiefs covering their heads and faces, leaving only their cruel eyes exposed.

The leader was quick to begin. He barked to one of his men, "Stay here and guard these two." To the remaining one he said, "Follow me. We two will search this place."

The two filed out of the room, but the mother cried out, "Wait."

Slowly the two returned.

"Please," she asked. "Let me wake up the children and bring them here."

"Why?" growled one of the intruders.

The mother offered her explanation. She spoke hurriedly, tumbling the words out. "You might make noise searching for loot. You will probably go searching into their rooms. Surely they will wake up and scream, then you might hurt them."

The gang leader was in a hurry to get this job done with. He wanted to get on his way because dawn was fast approaching, but he reluctantly gave his consent.

"You stay here. I'll send the maid."

The trembling maid was escorted by one of the thugs to the children's bedrooms. One by one she woke them. Bewildered and frightened, they were led to their waiting parents.

"Satisfied?" the leader asked with a leer. Without waiting for an answer, he quickly turned to his companion. "OK, let's go." Over his shoulder he said to the remaining one, "Watch them well."

The gunman made them all sit on the side of the bed. Then he relaxed, his back against the wall, and lit a cigarette.

"This will be a simple job," he thought. "What is it to guard a paunchy, middle-aged man and his family?"

Then a strange thing happened. The master leaped.

Certainly, the chances of survival were very slim. Maybe it was the fury at seeing his home invaded and his wife and children being treated so. The wife and the children, if they had it in their power, would certainly have willed him not to do so. What if they did take everything in the house? There was always a fresh start.

But whatever made him do it, no one knows. He saw the chance and swiftly he struck. He grabbed the gunman's hand, the one holding the pistol. His other arm slid around the thug's body in a vise-like grip. The man was held helpless. Wild-eyed and frantic, he fired a melee of shots into the ceiling.

This attracted the other men and they burst simultaneously into the room. Instantly they grasped the situation and poured five shots into the helpless man's body, miraculously missing his wife who was heroically aiding her husband.

Then like the cowards they were, they fled into the night.

Stumbling, he fell against his wife who gradually and painfully eased him to the floor, laying his head on her lap.

But it was too late; two shots had been fatal. Death was approaching swiftly.

"Oh, my God ... I'm heartily sorry ... for having offended thee ..."

Together they tried to recite the Act of Contrition, but it was never finished. The master's head slumped back into his wife's lap. His eyes had already begun to glaze and she burst out sobbing.

Thus perished the finest man I have ever known. He was a tribute to his country. A symbol of courage and decency to his friends. Loved, honored and cherished by his family.

I should know. He was my father.

What the old man remembers is different from what the boy wrote fifty years earlier. His memories of that night begin as he is shaken awake. He opens his eyes to see a man bending over him. The man's face is covered by two white hand-kerchiefs, one tied around his forehead and flipped backwards over his hair, the other tied across the bridge of his nose to hide his face, leaving only a slit that reveals his eyes. He remembers thinking in those first confused moments that Blanca, the family dog, was having her puppies and he was being called to watch.

He remembers being led to his parents' bedroom, where his mother and father are seated on the bed, just to the right of the door. He remembers seeing another man in the room with his parents, handkerchiefs also hiding his face. The man tells him to sit and the boy sits on the floor next to his mother and father, his back resting against the bed.

He remembers seeing his father stand up suddenly and lunge at the man, clutching him around the waist, grabbing at the wrist of the hand that holds the gun. He remembers watching the two of them struggle, sees the man shoot his gun at the ceiling.

He can't remember whether he is standing now or still sitting, but he is very close to the two men locked in their frantic embrace because he remembers the puzzled, plaintive look on his father's face as he grapples with the gunman, as if asking himself, "Why did I do this? What do I do now?"

He remembers his mother holding desperately onto his father as he struggles, pleading with him. "Sit down, Stanley, sit down, let him go," and saying to the man with the gun, "He doesn't mean it, he'll sit down, he doesn't mean it," then again to his father. "Let him go. Stanley, let him go, please let him go, it will be all right." He remembers this most of all.

"Mrs. Fisher was helping her husband, biting at the gangster," one news-paper reporter wrote the following day, but that's not what the old man remembers, because he can still see his father's stricken eyes, can hear his mother's pleading voice. And that is all he remembers of that night.

He doesn't know whether he turned away or chose to forget the rest of what he saw. But he doesn't remember his father being shot, doesn't see him fall, doesn't see him die.

There is a picture in his mind of the dead man lying in the bedroom on that night long ago, but it comes from a black-and-white photo in one of the news clippings that he waited fifty years to read. In the grainy image, preserved on yellowing newsprint, his father lies on his back, feet bare under striped pajama bottoms and a light-colored bathrobe. His left leg is bent, the knee propped on the wall against which he must have fallen before slumping to the floor. His face is turned toward the camera, but the features are obscured in the shadow of a dresser. Only a dark stain extending down the left shoulder and across the upper chest of the light bathrobe is plainly evident.

"Against the five masked gunmen," reads the caption under the photo, "Mr. C. S. Fisher had no chance."

The September 18, 1946, issue of *The Evening Herald*, Manila's English-language newspaper, carried this front-page account of the crime:

Briton Killed by
Five Gunmen
in Pasay Home

Cornelius Stanley Fisher, manager of the Specialty Corporation and a native of London, was riddled with bullets in his bedroom at 923 F. B. Harrison, Pasay, at around 3:15 this morning by five unknown men who broke into his residence to rob.

In the investigation conducted by Detectives P. Penaranda, C. Lagadi and D. Tugade of the homicide section, it was disclosed that five unknown men entered the house by cutting the wire screen of the window at the kitchen.

Pio Teves, the houseboy, who sleeps in the kitchen, woke up because of the commotion, but before he could call for help, one of the men pressed a revolver behind him and ordered him to keep quiet and to lead the malefactors to the room of Fisher.

Two of the unknown men stayed on the ground floor to act as guards while the remaining three went up with Teves who brought them to Fisher. Fisher, at the sight of the men in his room, tried to reach for his .45 caliber revolver which was grabbed by the robbers.

The family of Fisher was herded into the room with a lone armed guard while the two ransacked the rooms for loot. It was at this juncture that Fisher grappled with his guard for the possession of the firearm. The pistol in the course of the struggle went off attracting the robbers who were busy taking loot.

The robbers went into the room to help their companion and they riddled Fisher with bullets, killing him instantly.

Found missing from the Fisher household after the hoodlums had fled were P300 cash money, Fisher's .45 caliber pistol and personal papers.

Cornelius Stanley Fisher, who is a British subject, has his office at the Wilson Building at Juan Luna. Fisher is survived by his wife, Mercedes DeOcampo Fisher, 45, and five children.

Putting down the faded newspaper clipping, the old man picked up the phone and called his bank to inquire about the U.S. dollar-Philippine peso exchange rate. A clerk told him it was currently .02612 and offered to do the math for him. A few moments later she said, "At today's rate, 300 pesos is worth $7.84."

"Why did he do it—die so pointlessly?" the old man asked himself, then remembered overhearing the reason his mother gave someone a long time ago: "His favorite expression was 'My home is my castle.' He said it often. He died because he loved his family, because he was English and he was proud and he loved his family. That's why he died."

———————

And so I rose and went to my Innisfree by the sea.

There the memories found me. But not all of them. Some have vanished forever.

An everlasting regret is that I never asked my mother to tell me about herself and my father, about our family and the early times of our life together. In her last painful months, it would have been an act of kindness and grace for me to have sat and listened to her tell me about the halcyon years in Hong Kong and Manila.

But she is gone, and there are things I will never know, because knowing wasn't important until it became too late. And I am left with what I can remember. Now I yearn to tell my children so much more than what I know about this strong, complex, courageous woman, but I can't and their loss is as great as mine.

It took me nearly half a century to learn exactly what happened in those early morning hours of September 17, 1946. Here at the beach, I finally allowed myself to read the yellowed, crumbling newspaper clippings my mother had preserved in a cardboard scrapbook, along with the telegrams and letters of condolence she had received.

I had never asked to see them. I had never wanted to.

After my mother died of cancer in a New York City hospital in the winter of 1981, I took the scrapbook back to Oregon with me, along with thirteen single-spaced pages she had typed out in her bed during her last pain-ridden months. She had written them for her grandchildren, she had said. Those pages tell of her life in Manila and Hong Kong, and they are priceless to me now.

But after she died, I hid the words away, along with the clippings. I couldn't bear to look at them. I didn't, for another twenty years.

At the beach, the old man finally allows himself to remember, to accept, and forgive yet another denial as great as the boy's disavowal of his father's death—his lifelong repudiation of himself in search of someone he would never find, the person he could never be.

He remembers words he once read, what another Eurasian author said about her own yearning for acceptance: "Everywhere I belong, and everywhere I'm an outsider."

He remembers a story his Filipino mother told him when he was a boy in Manila, a story his English father had laughed at heartily. "When God created man," his mother said. "God fashioned a figure out of clay and stuck it in the oven. But God took it out too soon. And the white man was born. So God tried again, but this time left the clay figure in too long. And the black man was born. Then God tried once more and took him out exactly on time. And the brown man was born."

So the boy learned that God finally got it right on the third try.

But as a U.S. Marine stationed in the Deep South in 1957, he discovered a different set of partialities.

After his graduation from boot camp at Parris Island, South Carolina, the young man was assigned to the Second Marine Division at Camp Lejeune, North Carolina. Soon afterwards, he and another marine, who also had enlisted in New York City and gone through boot camp with him in the same platoon, visited a town near the sprawling base.

As the two PFCs were about to enter a restaurant in the small rural community, a man blocked their way. After peering intently at both, he told the twenty-two-year-old English-Filipino Marine from Manila, "You can come in." To the nineteen-year-old African-American Marine from the Bronx, he said, "*You* can't." Both men left quietly.

That evening, back at the base, the two were told a saying that they would hear many times again. "Around here," another Marine cautioned them, "if you're white, you're all right. If you're brown, you can hang around. If you're black, stand back."

The Eurasian Marine had come to America when he was eighteen, dispatched from a distant land to a Catholic boarding school for his senior year of high school, in a far-different culture peopled no longer in familiar shades of brown and tan but in starkly contrasting tones of white and black.

He arrived at the most vulnerable time of his life, not man or boy but something in-between, feeling lost and separate, excruciatingly alone—neither white nor black nor brown but an ambiguous alloy of indeterminate origin, desperately wanting to blend in and belong, to be simply, indistinguishably *American*.

At the beach, fifty years later, the old man understands finally that much of what he disavowed in himself before recognizing its irretrievable value, most of the heartache he caused himself and those who chose to love him, came out of that repudiation of his true self.

Such is the power of denial, the old man now realizes: a comforting ally in our struggles for survival, a fierce foe in our quest for ourselves. Denial finds us when we feel most alone, and only alone can we banish this demon that bars the long way home.

Chapter Five

The Unabashed Joys
of Self-Indulgence

I belonged first and foremost
to myself.
—Charlotte Wolffe

In our liberated age of happily never-marrieds and resolutely never-remarrieds, as increasingly more Americans trade in the traditional joys of partnering for happily-ever-aftering alone, contented singles such as Atlanta accountant Kate Wallace are asking, "What does being married have to do with having a terrific life?"

Certainly, there are things that can't be done alone, events and occasions in which we must seek from others what we cannot provide for ourselves. Carrying both ends of a long ladder comes to mind. As does ballroom dancing. And the horizontal mambo. It still takes two to tango, on the dance floor as well as in the bedroom.

Now, partners by their very definition ("persons who share or are associated with one another") are committed to giving one another as much as they receive, or they should be. It's the essential rule of successful coupling. The trouble is, one often winds up with the lion's share of giving, and the other the lion's share of getting.

"He hit me. Once."

It is Kathy Probst's terse reply to my question, an ominous beat strung between the two staccato sentences. I had asked her why she divorced after only ten months of marriage. She was twenty-two at the time, he was a year older, both of them still in college. She never remarried, says the flight attendant, now fifty-four, although there was a time in her life when she had more "roommates" than she can remember.

"That first mistake taught me never to just 'jump in' again," Probst continues. "If a man got serious, I ran the other way. I've always felt my life was full enough. I never felt the pressure to try again. By the time I was thirty, I realized how truly alone I was. It was then that I started getting this 'attitude' about myself and being alone."

"Bouncing around the way I did, moving from city to city, working all kinds of shifts, I realized I didn't really 'know' anyone except for a few high school classmates, and we weren't very close. I felt most out of place in Chicago," she reveals. "The city is very family-oriented."

Probst stops, laughs. "I went to church there once," she goes on. "Women grabbed their husbands' arms and stared. 'They have few single friends,' the minister told me later, apologetically."

The memory brings recollections of her brief union thirty years earlier. "I didn't like being married," she says stiffly. "I realized it within months, weeks even. He said he wanted kids, a happy little housewife, all of us doing things together. 'That's not what I want,' I thought almost immediately. Not every person is meant to get married—or have children. I'm happy with my life," she stresses.

What does she like about it? The freedom, the independence, the selfishness, Probst replies.

"Sure, single people get selfish—I use the word advisedly," says the University of California M.B.A., who worked for a large chemical company before embarking on her twenty-five-year career as a flight attendant for a major airline. "You don't share with anyone for one simple reason—you don't have to."

"You don't *plan* to become selfish, it just happens. Because you're alone, with no commitments, with only yourself to please, you learn to do everything you want to do for as long as you want to do it."

"You might say selfishness becomes a lifestyle. Anything different almost throws you off," she adds.

"Contrary to popular opinion, people who live alone usually have long to-do lists because they've had the time to develop many diverse interests. It's wonderful when you realize there are so many things you can do by yourself that you can't do in a relationship.

"I can get on a plane and fly to a city I've never been to just to walk around. I can do needlepoint for six to eight hours at a time, then go seven or eight months without touching it again. I can get completely into the projects I choose, whether it's reading or becoming computer literate or shopping antique malls or taking trips. Everyone who's single gets lonely at times, so we learn to develop interests to fill that loneliness.

"People who don't have a lot of interests because they've never had the time to indulge them find they have a problem when they finally get the time for themselves. Women, for instance, who build their lives around their husbands and children literally fall apart when that life is suddenly gone."

That wasn't the case with her mother, Probst recalls. "She was a musician and editor of a fine arts magazine who wrote plays on the side. So she was able to cope with my father being an alcoholic and extremely abusive at times. The life she built apart from him kept them together. The last two years before his death he gave up drinking, and they were the best two years of their lives. I like to think of those last years as my mother's reward for seeing the marriage through, bad as it got. And it was the life she built apart from him that kept them together, that allowed her to survive."

"When you're alone, you find you don't need one special person to have a good life," Probst sums up. "You can do it with many people. And you *should*."

Does she think she'll marry again? Probst ponders the question, shrugs her shoulders, answers finally: "I don't know. I haven't been looking for a long time. If it happens, fine, I guess. If not, that's fine too. I hate it when friends ask—and keep asking, 'Have you met anyone interesting lately?' I usually answer, 'Yeah, lots.' And I leave it at that."

"One thing I know for sure. Each year that I don't get married I know it will be harder to find someone. Because I don't know how much I'll be willing to give up in exchange for what I'll be getting. Some call it being 'set in your ways.' I call it selfishness—and it's highly addictive."

Would she do things differently if she were married now? "Absolutely," Probst replies.

"People who marry when they're in their forties, fifties, and sixties bring much more openness to the relationship. Each has to accept the other's quirky ways, learn to give each other the time and space both have gotten used to and can't get along without now. It's important to admit you're looking for a caring, comfortable companion rather than a romantic, highly sexual partner. It's also important not to try to change the other person," Probst adds.

"That's good advice regardless of your age, but I think it becomes crucial as you get older. You *have* to accept each other's eccentricities because no one's going to change. She talks to her cats—well, that's OK! He goes for long stretches of time without saying anything—tell yourself it's better than him never shutting up. He snores—hey, you probably do too. No reason you can't have separate bedrooms at your age.

"Give each other the luxury of time and space you've both come to treas-ure after so many years alone. Recognize it's a close, supportive friendship you're after—not a marriage in the classic sense of the word. You probably couldn't handle a marriage, but a deep friendship might be just the thing—for *both* of you."

Living alone again after two marriages, Alexis Padfield, sixty-one, lists her greatest pleasure as no longer having to have a set routine for herself. Her second-greatest pleasure, she says, is not having to be responsible for any-one but herself.

"I'm free to be totally myself in an unlimited manner," Padfield says gleefully.

"I—and *only* I—choose when to rise and when to retire each day, what to cook and when to eat, how long to be away from home and when I want to return, how I decorate my house, landscape my yard, and spend my money, when and where I vacation and with whom. My best new friend is *myself*," she makes clear.

"I've taken to giving this adorable creature the luxury of pedicures, massages, and facials. I let her soak in the tub as long as she wants, stay up all hours reading or watching TV in bed—all without the slightest guilt. Only after one has experienced the ups and downs, the highs and lows, the obligations and commitments of living with a partner can one truly know the deep joy of living alone," Padfield says.

"The subconscious desire for a mate shifts to a deep appreciation for meaningful friendships. I've always had an adventurous spirit and a zest for living. I've tried to accept change as an opportunity for growth, and so my periods of aloneness have rewarded me by expanding my self-awareness and appreciation for life. And I believe the future holds continuing opportunities for self-realization and the further unfolding of my creativity.

"As the static clears and space opens through my joy and awareness of living in the present, I feel my creative soul's desire for expression. No longer having to make lists and live for the future, I give myself the freedom to just allow the day to unfold. Time seems to have expanded and shortened at the same time," she says.

"I have more time for pleasure. Or is it simply that I find more pleasure in my daily activities? Yet, with my heightened sense of limited time, I want to grab hold of all that gives me pleasure, to revel in the joy of my *uniqueness*."

"I have fallen in love with my dog. This happened almost accidentally, as though I woke up one morning and realized: Oops! I'm thirty-eight and I'm single, and I'm having my most intense and gratifying relationship—with a dog. But we all learn about love in different ways, and this way happens to be mine."

The words are Caroline Knapp's, from her delightful book, *Pack of Two: The Intricate Bond Between People and Dogs*, in which she traces the historical shift in canine roles from working animals to family companions to emotional nurturers.

Knapp tells how she visited a Boston animal shelter to bring home an eight-week-old shepherd mix named Lucille. Both her parents had died, she reveals, and she had quit drinking eighteen months earlier, ending a twenty-year relationship with alcohol.

In a haze of uncertainty, Knapp agonized over who she was without her parents and without alcohol, how she would make her way in the world without access to either, how she could find new comfort in the face of her daunting vulnerability. A dog proved to be the fundamental answer to all her troubled questions.

"In her," Knapp writes, "I have found solace, joy, a bridge to the world."

Half of you are probably murmuring *Yes! Yes! Yes!* right about now, while the other half are making that familiar circular motion with a forefinger in the vicinity of your temples.

For there are dog lovers and there are cat lovers and there are those who consider the first two groups to be a bit off plumb.

Which is why Knapp warns against revealing the depth of your feelings about Fluffy or Fido, regardless of how powerful the attachment, how rewarding the union, how sustaining the relationship.

Do so, she cautions, and you stand accused of ascribing human attributes to a pet, which is naive. Of substituting animal love for human love, which is perverse. Of sublimating the desire for a spouse and family into the adoration of a pooch, which is pathetic. Worst of all, you risk hearing those most condescending of non–pet-owner words: *Oh, please, it's just a dog.*

Well, yeah, that's the whole point.

It's *because* they're dogs, because they're what we can't be, as hard as we try, that we cherish their virtues. It's why we idealize and extol their unfailing loyalty, patience, nobility, courage, selflessness, and devotion—so exemplary in them, so elusive in ourselves.

Want perfect love? Try heaven. The closest thing to it you'll find on earth is a dog.

That's why 50 percent of respondents in a 1999 American Animal Hospital Association survey said they would "very likely" risk their lives to rescue their pets. Thirty-three percent said they would be "somewhat likely," while 13 percent said "not very likely," and 4 percent said "not likely."

It's why 21 percent of them carry photos of their pets in their wallet or purse. And why 57 percent of pet-owners said in a 1996 survey that if they were stranded on a desert island, they'd want a pet as their only companion.

Knapp acknowledges another common view about us—that we turn to our animals for love and affection by default because the "real" thing is so hard to come by in our fractured, isolated, alienating world. And maybe there's truth to that. But so what?

"Love is love," is how Paula, a forty-six-year-old L.A. author, puts it. "I don't care if it comes from humans or from animals: it's the same feeling." Still, it bothers many of us that the human variety often pales beside the canine kind.

But that's not a sad commentary on our modern culture, Knapp points out. It's simply the nature of "the remarkable, mysterious, often highly complicated dances that go on between individual dogs and their owners. The dance is about love," she says.

"It's about attachment that's mutual and unambiguous and exceptionally private, and it's about a kind of connection that's virtually unknowable in human relationships because it's essentially wordless."

One of my greatest joys at the beach has come from the open-ended time I've been able to spend with my dog, a privilege and pleasure that the exigencies of living, working, and raising a family in the city denied me. Being together virtually every moment of every day these past five years has forged bonds no two humans could possibly achieve. That's only my opinion, of course, but I don't think two people could spend every moment of every day together without desperately needing a break. But you can do it—gloriously—with a dog.

And if you tell me that what I feel for him can't possibly be as strong and vivid and deep as what I've felt for the other loves of my life, then it's my turn to make that familiar circular motion with a forefinger in the vicinity of my temple.

"I'm rarely unhappy when I'm moving briskly, breathing deeply, and stretching my body," Elise Whitely replies when asked what she does to nurture herself.

"I've always used vigorous activity to deal with my emotions. When I need to get focused, to think something through or solve a problem, the best way for me is to put on my running shoes and get in some miles. Sometimes I'll listen to music, but I've found that it can interfere with the solutions popping into my head, so I usually prefer to exercise in silence."

Friends are another way she nurtures herself, says Whitely, sixty-one, who has been single for the past fourteen years after a twenty-year marriage. She tells about a thank-you note she just received for a kindness she had done. The grateful person had written: "A friend is a gift you give yourself, and today I gave myself you."

The words touched her deeply, Whitely says, "because that's how I think of my friends, as wonderful gifts I give myself."

She's always had the knack of being a good friend to men—*just* friends, she emphasizes, even to the married ones.

"Their wives don't seem threatened," Whitely says proudly. "They don't get jealous, even though I do receive signals of envy—the feeling they wish they were single, too." She grins impishly.

"But maybe it's just my imagination because I'm so happy not being married anymore."

She thinks she's a good friend to men and not threatening to their wives, Whitely points out, because she resists the urge to pass on gossip or to be judgmental. "At my age I know I can't change my friends, so I don't try," she says.

"I think it's the secret of being a true friend—not trying to 'fix' anyone else but yourself, just letting them *be* so they can fix themselves in their own time and space. If they become annoying or withdrawn, I 'give them a rest' and go spend time with others."

Also paramount in her self-nurturing regimen is the strict maintenance of her good health, she says. "I'm almost evangelical about physical exercise. That doesn't mean I stint on my medical insurance, but I take a lot of preventive measures in order to stay healthy and uninjured so I don't have to use my insurance." And one of those measures, she points out, is eating wisely so she doesn't gain weight. "I can't keep from getting old," Whitely says.

"But I don't have to get fat. Living alone, I can breakfast on last night's salad. I have complete control over my own body—what I do with it and what I put into it, which is probably why I still weigh what I did when I was in high school."

As for staying uninjured, she passes along a personal motto: "When you live alone, never walk around in the dark, climb tall ladders, or get on the roof!"

Patience is also on her self-nurturance list. "I've noticed all my favorite people are patient," she says. "They're patient with themselves. They're patient with nature. They're patient with their grandchildren and with their friends. They're patient with life in general."

"They don't sweat the small stuff. They give everything enough time to work itself out—and it always does. They don't get angry when they fail and usually give themselves—and others—a second chance. They're tolerant and kind and forgiving. I nurture myself by trying to be like them."

Now that he's older, William Carrington relishes the peace and quiet of his alone time, the total "soundlessness" of his own company, because it reinforces the feeling of inner serenity he now possesses.

"The only sounds I hear are the ones I make," says the sixty-five-year-old New York adman who retired to Cape Cod. "What a luxury! For so much of our early adulthood, sound is such an incessant part of our lives: family voices—talking, fighting, yelling—the yakkety-yak of fellow workers, the blare of car radios, elevator music, the TV that someone in the house always seems to have on. Even rational conversation around the dinner table seemed noisy except during parent-enforced silences, which hardly ever worked."

Living alone also provides the voluptuous opportunity to indulge his "eccentricities" and "little habits" freely, adds Carrington. "When I'm alone, the toothpaste cap always goes back on the tube. I always know where the flashlight is. I can go to a bookshelf and immediately find that special book. I can be sure my favorite blue shirt is in the closet—exactly where I put it weeks ago."

When he returned from a recent four-month visit to Florida, he says, some of his "challenges" were hunting for his favorite paring knife, finding the unfinished magazine he'd set aside for safekeeping, tracking down the supply of three-way light bulbs he thought he'd stored in the hall closet but now weren't there. "How pleasurable life can be," he muses, "when the most demanding tasks of one's day are so pleasantly inconsequential."

And though traveling with others offers the joy of immediately shared discoveries and the pleasures of comradeship, being a solitary sojourner has much to offer as well, he says.

"You can march to your own drummer—*all* the time. If you want to give that museum five minutes instead of four hours, fine! If you feel like taking the subway instead of a taxi, there's no one to complain. If you really want to walk through that little neighborhood of tiny shops, even though it's raining, you don't have to worry about dragging a complaining companion along. Or feel guilty about leaving someone alone in the hotel room.

"And you can forget about the 'Well, where shall we go for dinner tonight?' routine and all it entails. If you really feel like a McDonald's fix— and you're in Paris—you just go."

Cynthia Meier describes her second marriage, which ended when she was thirty-two, as "four years of wedded bliss, one year of severe struggling." And for three years after the divorce she "hung on like a pit bull," says the forty-five-year-old operating room nurse—trying to retrieve the relationship with her physician ex-husband.

"I was desperate," says Meier. "I felt I'd be nothing without him."

Her first marriage to an "extremely liberal yuppie," when both of them were twenty-one, lasted half as long. The two men in her life, though poles apart in their professional and political orientations—the first, a left-wing social activist; the second, an ultraconservative cardiovascular surgeon— were predictably similar in what drew her to them, says Meier:

"I've always been attracted to high-powered men—strong, opinionated, extroverted, egocentric dynamos who stirred things up, brought excitement to my life, made me think. 'Hey, that's who I am as well.'

"When I was married, I made each of my husband's politics my own, as radically different as they were. I wound up giving my complete self to both of them, surrendering my entire individuality. I took up each one's entire persona—lock, stock, and barrel—and gladly, because I didn't feel I had one of my own."

Single and in therapy these past thirteen years, Meier still has one major issue to resolve but isn't certain she ever will. She has a great job, she says, along with the trust and respect of her peers, a strong relationship with her parents, close connections to her siblings, and numerous friends—

> "It's taken me a long time to recognize who I am and to admire and value that person. I'm not going to give her up now—not for anyone, not ever again—because she's a wonderful, very real person worth hanging onto at all costs."

but no ability to forge an emotional bond with a man. She'd *like* to, she makes it clear, but not at the cost of surrendering her identity once more.

"Living alone," says Meier, "I've come to realize all those years spent with others were spent living an unauthentic life. It's taken me a long time to recognize who I am and to admire and value that person. I'm not going to give her up now—not for anyone, not ever again—because she's a wonderful, very real person worth hanging onto at all costs."

Meier has made her home a place of comfort and refuge where she always feels safe and in total control. Everything in her lakeside apartment—the furniture, fabrics, colors, artwork, accoutrements, and decor—all reflect *her* decorative tastes, *her* style, *her* artistic sensibilities, she stresses.

"I gave them all away when I catered totally to someone else's needs, someone else's preferences, someone else's desires—to the total exclusion of my own. I'm taking them back," she says triumphantly. "They're all for *me* now."

Meier feels particularly "hugged and nurtured" in her bedroom, she says. "When I moved into my new home after the divorce, I told myself I was going to do this right!"

She bought an antique four-poster bed, "the exact kind I've known I wanted since I was eight." She bought a new mattress and box springs, a state-of-the-art electric heating pad, a luxurious down comforter, a gaggle of down pillows, 200-count cotton sheets, an ideal nightstand, and a perfect reading lamp.

"When I was done," Meier says, "I had a *bedroom*. Much more than a place to sleep, though. it's a sanctuary in every sense of the word—a warm, comforting, serene place I'm always happy to go, where I'm perfectly content to be alone. In fact," she adds, "I'm beginning to wonder whether any man will be able to make me as happy and content in that bed as I've learned to make myself."

Chapter Six

The Dragon at the Gate
of Solitude: Loneliness

But now I find that solitude,
far from being the price,
is turning out to be the prize.
—ALIX KATES SHULMAN

"Being alone is better than *wanting* to be alone."

The words were posted in an Internet chat room by a recent divorcee. "Being alone," she then added, "is better than being in a relationship you hate and wanting to get out of it, but staying because you don't want to be alone. Having someone around when you don't want them there is miserable. More miserable than being by yourself."

Norwegian actress Liv Ullman put it this way to a *New York Times* reporter: "I just think that sometimes it is less hard to wake up feeling lonely when you are alone than to wake up feeling lonely when you are with someone else. Some people would be better off alone, but they feel they've got to get hold of someone to prove they're worthwhile," Ullman added.

"If they do decide to be alone, part of their loneliness will come from outside, rather than inside [because] society will pity them, look down on them."

"There are lonely hours," conceded even that eloquent loner Edward Abbey. "There are times when solitaire becomes solitary, an entirely different game, a prison term, and the inside of the skull as confining and unbearable as the interior of the house trailer on a hot day."

"At every stage," affirms John Dunne, "the question is that of loneliness. The loneliness can hold one in the human circle; it can drive one into solitude; and it can deter one from returning to the human circle."

"Your pain is often the same as my pain." Leslie, thirty-four, consoled a woman whose journal entry on the Internet touched her deeply.

"No one loves me," Leslie wrote in response. "No one really did when I was little. My husband did a little, but was really incapable of loving deeply. I go through periods of intense, screaming loneliness—aloneness. What it eventually comes down to for me is that I want a mother and I never really had one and no one can give me one now. Apparently I have to grieve that loss and as I grieve, the pain will slowly get less. I am grieving and healing with the help of two wonderful therapists and my art and music and poetry and my own journal writing. It is getting better. I have no answers for you," Leslie concluded.

"I probably can't give you what you need, but I am willing to share some of my journey with you if you want me to. At the very least I can tell you that another shares a same kind of pain, and maybe that will help you feel less alone."

"Scared to death" of being alone, Cynthia Holmes tells about the devastating loneliness she is feeling. Even though she's lived an exciting life and has just returned home to Connecticut from Texas, her aloneness is being tested as never before.

"I'm a single mom and I just landed an awesome job in publishing," says Holmes, thirty-seven. "Physically, I'm in great shape and attractive. I have a family that loves me and friends who adore me. However, I still feel the loneliness. I loved Texas and wish I was still there." There was lots to do and plenty of people with whom to escape her loneliness, Holmes reasons, while Connecticut is very quiet and conservative. Still, she doesn't understand her feeling of intense loneliness.

"My family is trying hard to help me be happy, yet I feel scared and lonely. But I'm not depressed, just searching. I need to know I'm not the only one who feels this way. But this isn't about me anymore. I have a fifteen-year-old son who lives here, and I felt it was time to put my needs aside and move back so I'd be near him."

She also left an abusive relationship, Holmes says. "Not physical abuse but something worse—the mental kind that corrupts the spirit. And get this— I'm still thinking about him, still asking myself, 'What if?' So with the perfect surroundings I'm blessed with—a great job, healthy children—why can't I handle this feeling of emptiness and loneliness?" she asks herself.

"Every day since I've been back, I feel the challenge."

"It never crossed my mind I would be completely alone," says Bianca Lejon, forty-three. "That I'd leave my second husband and not have his replacement, that my children would follow their dreams and live their lives without my help, that I would live in a small city where I had no relatives, that I would be far away from my culture and my birthplace."

These thoughts crossed her mind, she says, as she drove past the home in which she had lived three years ago. Other hearts were enjoying its warmth now, other lives were making memories there. At one time the house had held her, her husband, their four children, her mother-in-law and two dogs.

"Where did all my roles go—mother, wife, daughter, and daughter-in-law?" she asked herself. "I never realized those times, those roles would pass, that I'd move on to the next stage of my life."

That dark stage, she says, is an empty house that embraces the depths of her loneliness. "There are days it swallows me up. There was a time I brought home a lover to relieve the pain, to distract me, but now the shadows are back in spite of my vain attempts. They mock me, whispering 'You fool, you can't get rid of us! We are the mother in you, the caregiver, the peacemaker. We are restless and will reappear each time you feel your emptiness.' It is so painful to live in the present," says the freelance writer and novelist.

"I yearn for the days when I was known by someone for more than a day, a week, or a month, when the thought of solitude never entered the picture. I'd be content now to be back in that house staring at my husband of sixteen years smoking his twentieth cigarette, watching a John Wayne movie for the hundredth time, recovering from his third stroke, grouchy, but who planted flowers and brought me their first blossoms, who fed our children when I couldn't be there, who would pat my ass when he was horny, and I would feel my instant sexual arousal.

"'Will my life reflect this passage as an emerging creation of new inner resources?' I ask myself. 'Will my womb give birth to new life, new dreams, new fulfillment?' These thoughts encircle my solitude as I slip beneath the covers and cry myself to sleep.

"It's all yet to come, I tell myself, and I need to adapt to a new script, new plots, new roles. The lights are on, the play has just begun as I come on stage, the audience awaits my first line and I, too, await my first word of grace."

Rita Vicente's "dream place to live," she says, has always been a tree house, a lighthouse, or a fire tower. In fact, reveals the former Forest Service employee, she spent many years working in federal wilderness areas and campgrounds.

"I was behind locked gates in the winter months," says Vicente, sixty-one, "and that was very special. I couldn't afford my own land, and this was the next best thing. All those years in the forest, alone most of the winters, I never had any fear. I worked all shifts, coming and going in the middle of the night on a little motorcycle. I'd walk six miles to work when I was snowed in, but mostly drove over ice-packed roads. I simply had faith in myself back then, always felt special somehow, protected. And I liked myself. I enjoyed my own company back in those quiet times."

Vicente recalls with particular nostalgia the isolated, snowbound campgrounds of her youth. "I spent those winters with the wildlife—mountain lions, coyotes, squirrels, and me," she recalls.

"One year my Christmas cards were a photo I'd taken of my footprints in the snow. The ponderosa pines, blanketed in white, magnificent, and so quiet after a snowstorm, were unbelievably wonderful—as was standing there looking at them. Just me in the stillness.

"I felt close to God. It was true serenity."

Three marriages have come and gone since then, she reveals. The first lasted eight years, the second five years, the third just five months.

"There was a quote, from Thoreau, I think it was, that I used to cherish, something about crows going in flocks and wolves in packs, but the lion and the eagle are solitaires. I kept those words in mind for many years. I didn't trust those who never gave themselves the chance to live alone and get to know themselves, who were *afraid* to be alone, and running from their aloneness."

> "I used to feel sorry for them, those people who cling to people. I always thought they brought more needs than gifts. I felt that if they didn't want to be by themselves, with themselves, I surely didn't want to be with them either."

"I used to feel sorry for them, those people who cling to people. I always thought they brought more needs than gifts. I felt that if they didn't want to be by themselves, with themselves, I surely didn't want to be with them either."

Vicente is quiet for a while. When she speaks again, her voice is sad, and so soft, I can barely hear her: "I felt sorry for them then, because I was never a clinger. But I can relate to them now because I've lost the feeling of closeness to myself, the serenity I once felt when I was alone. I used to relish my solitude, but not so much now. My isolation is engulfing me."

"Living alone does not make one lonely," says Roy Sharpe, thirty-nine. "Not in and by itself. I know many people who are married or living with significant others and *very* lonely. Worse, they feel trapped."

"Being alone doesn't make you lonely. Living an unproductive, self-centered, unloving, friendless life makes you lonely.

"Once we learn that life is not entirely about us, that it's about others as well, then we've taken a giant stride in overcoming loneliness and enjoying being alone. Whether you're married or living alone or with a friend or a lover, the more you focus on yourself, the more lonely you'll become."

———————

When I moved to Washington's North Beach Peninsula on New Year's Day 1994, I brought with me a book I was writing on the mental, emotional, and psychological challenges of working from home. At the beach, alone as I'd never been in my life, I struggled with one chapter in particular because it dealt with a demon I've grappled with as long as I can remember. If anything would kill me here, I figured, it would be loneliness.

Early in the chapter on befriending solitude I wrote: "Of all the obstacles to working alone, one towers above the rest—the psychological sumo wrestler of them all: loneliness."

A few pages later, I added this melancholy observation: "However you confront the specter of loneliness, know that it will stalk your electronic cottage. Know you may have to exorcise it occasionally, but don't fear this gray ghost of your solitude. It could become the best friend you ever had."

And I ended with a whistling-in-the-dark affirmation: "To fight isolation is to face adult life. It is crucial to being on your own, and the testing grounds are your mind and heart. Being on your own means being alone. It doesn't mean being lonely. Unless you let it."

Six years later I realize that most of the advice I offered involves staying firmly in touch with others, electronically or in person—paddling periodically from one's sheltered cove into the mainstream of humanity, lingering at rest stops along the way: a neighborhood bar or espresso shop where friends can be found and everybody knows your name. "Hospitable institutions of mediation between the individual and larger society," Ray Oldenburg calls them in his book, *Great Good Places.*

The trouble is, while great good places provide necessary respites from ourselves (not to mention requisite locations for TV sitcoms), they only provide reprieves from our loneliness. Perhaps not even that, for lonely people carry their sense of alienation into the very heart of convivial society—wherever they attempt to elude their insular selves.

Even though engulfed by bright lights, loud music, and bold revelers, the lonely remain pitifully aware that their emotional wasteland has nothing to do with other people, that it's entirely a condition of self—thus inescapable.

Escape, therefore, isn't the answer to loneliness, but *surrender*—total capitulation to that relentless despoiler of our solitude.

Surrender is also what Susan Baumgartner did, alone in the Idaho wilderness. The then-thirtysomething Seattle writer abandoned a promising career and metropolitan lifestyle to take up residence on 8.6 acres in the hinterlands of northern Idaho. Utterly alone in that desolate backcountry, she wrote in her book, *My Walden*:

"Loneliness, once the captor of my spirit, now seems like a dear companion and wears the gentler name of solitude. It happened slowly, gradually. Instead of fighting loneliness, I learned to take it inside of me and to fill it with thoughts and fantasies and plans. I structured it to be productive. I learned to count on its solid presence. It seems like I am never lonely anymore."

Kelly O'Rourke capitulated to her own dread of loneliness in a desolate island cabin. A constantly on-the-go Los Angeles film producer, who didn't want a romantic involvement but couldn't reconcile her desperate need for others, O'Rourke gave up her L.A. apartment, put everything she owned into storage, and moved with her two cats to a tiny island on Lake Kawaguesaga in Wisconsin's rugged north woods.

"I needed to depend on myself, to squash the need for *anyone*, and instead rely on and be comfortable with only me," she later described her showdown with loneliness in a *Cosmopolitan* article. "Only then could I again become the woman I knew myself to be—caring, giving, secure."

O'Rourke was successful. "Here on this resilient little island," she recorded her battle triumphantly, "I have weathered the storm, have made it through, kept company by a woman I'd traveled all these many miles to meet again. Myself."

Not so fortunate was Victoria Castanelli. Loneliness nearly killed her at the age of twenty-seven—by her own hand.

"One day I decided I didn't want to live anymore," she relates twenty years later. "I was alone for the first time in my life and it terrified me. I felt hopeless, afraid to face the future, convinced it only held disappointment and emptiness for me, so one afternoon I made up my mind to leave—for good."

Castanelli, now forty-seven, gathered up her important documents, jotted down the possessions she wanted specific people to receive, wrote a letter of apology to her parents, put the papers in a shoe box, laid it on the passenger seat of her car, plugged every hole in the garage she could reach, got into her '73 Datsun 240Z, turned on the ignition, and waited to die.

Twice married and twice divorced while she was in her early twenties, both marriages lasting two years, Castanelli had just broken up with two boyfriends, each of whom had found out about the other and promptly dumped her.

Describing herself as pretty, creative, talented, willful, and smart when she was young, she says she was a stranger to failure, rejection, and ridicule throughout her precocious childhood, teen years, and early adulthood. "I didn't learn about those things until later."

Raised by wealthy, loving parents who spoiled and indulged her, she had a photographic memory, Castenelli relates wistfully, received straight A's in school without effort, taught herself how to play the guitar, had a good singing voice and belonged to choral and acting groups, learned languages effortlessly, and excelled in French.

She was all set to spend her senior year of high school in France but didn't want to leave her boyfriend and chose virtually at the last minute not to go. It was her first huge regret, she says.

"That's when the trouble started. I found I couldn't be alone, that solitude was my worst enemy, a demon I couldn't bear to have around."

Castanelli went on to college, only to quit after her freshman year to marry for the first time. "I know now, without realizing it then," she says, "that I was *afraid* to be alone. There's no other word for it. I'd plan tons of activities, surround myself with people to make sure it never happened. I'd stay in awful relationships to avoid the depression I'd inevitably feel when I *was* alone. My father used to say I was 'in love with love,' and he was right. I was Cinderella, forever waiting to go to the ball. I've never been in love with a person, only with the euphoric high I've always associated with being *in* love."

As long as she can remember, says Castanelli, the men in her life have been the primary, essential validation of her worth and happiness, starting with her father, a family physician.

"Each time he saw me his face would light up. No one else mattered when I was in the room. He would always say yes after my mother had said no. He was always patient, kind, and supportive of everything about me, as was my mother, but it was my father around whom my universe revolved.

"Later, before and after my two divorces, I always had at least one man in my life—usually two, in case one left. I couldn't do without the constant attention and adulation that had become indispensable to my sense of well-being."

On that fateful afternoon in the garage, Castanelli says, she woke up wondering what she was doing in her car with the motor running. "I turned off the ignition, stumbled into the house, went upstairs, and got in bed. I was very tired. I was very stupid."

It was two days, she thinks, before her parents and one of her boyfriends—worried because she hadn't gone to work and didn't answer her phone—went to her house and found her, still in bed. She was alive but the carbon monoxide had taken its toll of brain cells, she says.

"I didn't know who or where I was and why I was there. I didn't recognize my boyfriend. I couldn't remember my age, what kind of work I did, what day or month or year it was, or almost anything else. My parents took me to live with them. I couldn't taste food. I had to be taken daily to my father's medical office for catheterization since my bowels wouldn't work.

"The messages from my brain had become scrambled. I used to have beautiful penmanship, but the words I scribbled were those of a child learning to write, ugly, barely decipherable. I slept most of the time, but when I was awake I'd ask my mother the same questions over and over: 'Why am I here?' 'Where do I work?' 'Who is my boyfriend?' 'How old am I?'

"My father made me write the answers over and over on a notepad by my bed, but each time I awoke I'd scream for my mother and ask her the same questions, again and again."

She was tested and retested, evaluated and reevaluated, Castanelli says. The prognosis was that she wouldn't improve. The recommendation: that she be placed in a nursing home—at the age of twenty-seven. "But my father knew my strong will. He told me the brain is a marvelous thing, that if I tried very hard I could train the healthy part of my brain to do what the damaged parts used to do, but I had to be willing to work harder than I'd ever worked in my life. I said I would."

The excruciating road back took years of effort, she says. "I practiced writing endlessly. I read and reread the same page of a book—over and over—only to return ten minutes later without being able to remember a single word. But I kept reading. Although I'd become shy and introverted—the complete opposite of everything I had been—I started seeing visitors, but then couldn't remember they had come. For the first time in my life I became sensitive to the feelings of others. And a good listener, someone who strained to hear and extract meaning from every word and took notes so she wouldn't forget the important things she was told."

"I'd fill in portions of a check before going into a store so I wouldn't have to ask what year it was. I left notes to myself in places I was sure to come across them again, reminders to myself there were 'clothes in washer' or 'macaroni and cheese in oven' so I wouldn't leave them rotting for weeks.

"I'd ask someone to go over my grocery lists and remove repetitive items. If not, I'd wind up with four or five half-gallons of milk in my cart, which made me embarrassed and angry at the checkout stand."

Castanelli joined the downtown YMCA and started exercising and running regularly to help her mind work better and to make new friends, she says.

"Most of them are successful professionals—executives, doctors, dentists, writers, and lawyers—who accepted me despite my handicap. They'd kid me about my memory, which helped a lot, saying things like, 'It's Vicky's fault—I told her three times.' Or 'Go ahead and talk about it—she won't remember anyway.'

"When something's my fault at work, I'm able to defuse the situation by joking about it, saying stuff like, 'Well, it couldn't have been *me*—everyone knows I have a steel-trap memory!'"

"Humor gets me through most difficult situations, and I thank God for it because an ongoing problem is that people think I'm normal because I *look* normal. But sometimes things just don't print because the machinery is gone. I accept that I have a severe brain deficit, and through the acceptance of others, I've learned to be all right with myself, who I am now, and my new life."

From painting newsstands at Goodwill during her lengthy vocational rehabilitation period, through the countless menial jobs she held for mere days or weeks before being fired, Castanelli has progressed to a responsible clerical position with a large federal agency. She recently received another promotion, she says.

"The people I work with accept my limitations and help me build on my strengths. I keep a daily log that reads like a diary and functions as a substitute brain. I make enough money to support myself, I'm putting something away for the future. And I enjoy life."

Then Castanelli adds something startling: "Even though I could be making a lot more money had I not tried to end my life, I wouldn't trade all the things I have for what I had and who I was before that crazy day twenty years ago. People say they like me better now. I know I like and appreciate *them* a lot more, particularly my poor parents whom I put through so much pain. The only way I can repay them is by becoming the person they'd hoped I would be," she says.

"Life is wonderful now because of the little things—nothing particularly intense or male-oriented the way it always had to be. Before, I could have had a fistful of goodies and still be whining about what I didn't have.

"Happiness now is being with my family, visiting with a friend, waking up to the realization I have a job, remembering what I did yesterday, being able to taste my food, to go to the bathroom by myself. Happiness is helping others.

"It's accomplishing tasks that are difficult but were once impossible, reading a book and remembering what I read. Its being able to learn, especially from the challenges each new day provides—and seeing those challenges, not as adverse situations but as opportunities for growth.

"Happiness is accepting myself and my life with all its limitations and possibilities. Happiness is *living*. 'Is that *me* talking?' I sometimes ask myself, and exultantly hear myself reply, '*Yes!*'"

We each have our journey to our true self, and each of us must make it alone. I know that now. All those years I fled my loneliness in search of others, I waited for myself on a lonely beach.

And if I choose to return to others, it will be because the things they can give me are more important than the things I can give myself.

What matters most is that I've found the essence of who I am—that, first and foremost, I belong to myself. Knowing that I'm all right with myself, *by* myself, I know I'll be all right with others, anywhere I choose to be.

My emotional well-being comes with a lifelong warranty that allows me to go anywhere I choose alone. instead of forever being bound to the people, places, and things I used to find indispensable to my sense of security and self-worth.

And yet I worry sometimes about my deliberate aloneness. Am I protesting too bravely my newfound equanimity in solitude? By turning to myself, have I given up on everyone else?

Have I erected my seclusion as a shield against further pain and disappointment, thrown in the towel of life, and begun a quiet, fearful withdrawal from life itself, from the human commitment and involvement society decrees is its essence?

Perhaps.

But I'm resolved to explore this undiscovered country fully, to see how deep, how far my inward journey will take me, for my only hope of finding my place in the world, I know, is to find myself.

Chapter Seven

Alone Together: Making the Best of Both Worlds

I would be married,
but I'd have no wife;
I would be married
to a single life.
—JAMES GRAHAM

"I don't try to live *his* life with him," Holly Merrill describes her ten-year marriage to Richard Knocks. "I try to live *my* life with him."

The greatest gift they give each other, says Merrill, is the permission to be themselves. Together.

Knocks, fifty-seven, sums up their outwardly improbable but inwardly satisfying relationship in this fashion: "None of us is a complete human being. Each of us is strong in some ways and deficient in others. All of us have developed certain areas of ourselves and allowed others to atrophy. But others can give us what we've neglected to give ourselves. They can help stimulate those things of quality in us that shouldn't wither. That's what we do for each other."

> "All of us have developed certain areas of ourselves and allowed others to atrophy. But others can give us what we've neglected to give ourselves. They can help stimulate those things of quality in us that shouldn't wither."

Divorced in 1986 after a twenty-two-year marriage, Merrill, fifty-five, says that her first husband—a handsome, gregarious research physician, who ran marathons on the side—was "terrific" with others. "He was someone who gave it all away, then would come home empty, wanting to be filled. I was very lonely living with him. I'm not lonely with Dick. In contrast to my first husband, he's nurturing, solid, stable, always here for me. How I feel about Dick isn't nearly as important as how I feel about myself when I'm with him," Merrill adds. "That's the best way to judge a relationship. Do you like the person *you* are when you're with him?"

Her husband, she says, is introverted to the point that their life together excludes virtually everyone else. Still, it's one of the reasons she was attracted to him, she reveals. "He didn't bring a lot of baggage in the form of family or business or social obligations. As a person who truly liked being alone, he lived his entire adult life as an urban hermit. He never married or had children. His only relatives are elderly parents living in Florida and a sister in California. I became his major focus. And that is very appealing. What's more, he's thoughtful, attentive, considerate, a wonderful listener, and totally committed to me. He's extremely easy to live with—not good socially," she concedes, "but tremendous one-on-one with me, which is all that counts."

"He isn't jealous or possessive, doesn't make emotional or sexual demands, never makes me feel guilty about saying no to anything. Perhaps we balance each other. Dick is thoughtful, conservative, dependable, predictable, precise, detail-oriented, does things slowly, doesn't take to 'newness' easily, isn't one to jump into anything without carefully thinking it through. I'm pretty much the opposite, a lot more spontaneous, seldom thinking about the consequences of my impetuousness, just doing it!"

They met around the time of her divorce, Merrill relates, and slowly developed a strong friendship before they married five years later. "I brought all the baggage," she says, "an ex-spouse and two daughters for him to put up with, a house with a huge yard that we own jointly and is very much of a mixed blessing for him. It's the first time he's owned a house," she explains.

"He lived his whole adult life in cheap apartments with minimum furniture and possessions, pursuing a lifestyle patterned on Thoreau's. He doesn't like the routine of caring for things because he's never gone along with the traditional values of society, and now there's always something to be done at home that takes him away from his reading and poetry writing.

"Sometimes I wonder if it's all worth it for him. I urge him to go off by himself, as I do. You need to strike a balance, I tell him, do things with others, but he has limited tolerance for socializing and a very loyal sense of family, so I try not to pressure him too much."

"So what we have in common," Merrill says, "is our house, our evening ritual of dinner followed by a walk with the dog and sleeping together." Once a month they go to a contra dance, occasionally a movie in town. They do make an occasional trip together, maybe one a year—the last to Utah to go camping.

"Our social life," she says, "is entirely of my creation. Dick is rarely inclined to initiate activities, even with me, probably due to his ingrained pattern of living alone. I feel like the engine pulling him out of himself into the world, and I sometimes I resent this. I feel like I have two lives," Merrill continues.

"One as a single person, going hiking, skiing, backpacking, attending lectures and slide shows, taking part in potluck lunches and song circles in different homes. I often travel by myself to other states to hike and bike with touring groups. My great love is being outdoors—doing anything and everything that can be done outside. Dick doesn't begrudge my going away. I, in turn, allow him the personal space to be what *he* is." There's a lot of separation deliberately built into the marriage, she says.

"He lived so much of his life alone that it was a huge step for him to move in with me, so we've developed certain house rules, so to speak, that make him more comfortable. They're a way for him to preserve his space, his identity and individuality. Each of us, for instance, regards the other's privacy as paramount. Neither touches anything the other leaves lying around—what's his is his, what's mine is mine.

"He keeps his own money; I keep mine. He does his own laundry; I do mine. We each buy our own groceries. We alternate cooking dinner and each of us does it with our own food."

Merrill describes her partner's daily routine: "He takes walks, but mostly he spends the time in his den, reading endlessly and writing his poetry—with no TV, radio, or coffee to divert him. He's been able to exist without colleagues or friends, also without recognition or encouragement, without any outward validations of success," she adds with quiet admiration.

"He does it on his own internal strength. He's never been published but goes on happily writing his poetry for his own sake, getting up to face the world and live his life without any external aids or resources. I think it's remarkable."

And yet, she says, wistfulness creeping back into her voice, "living with a hermit isn't easy. Being with someone who creates his own world, internally, and has such different values from our society and culture is a challenge. People tend to see their partners as validations of themselves socially, and yet each of us is so highly individual. Also, I was much more isolated when Dick and I first met, and a different dynamic has been created between us. I've changed much more than he has," Merrill goes on.

"I think his introversion has pushed me in the opposite direction, and I've become more outgoing. He doesn't resent this, for which I'm grateful. Partly due to his nurturing, I've grown a lot stronger in our years together. I've taken on more challenges, become more involved in teaching and various community and art activities. I've also been going to a counselor to help resolve some of my issues. Even though it wasn't couples therapy, I think it's helped our marriage."

Merrill laughs. "You might say our motto is 'Live and let live.' But our life together affirms that the things two very different people can give each other are more important than the things they can't give," Merrill sums up. "And that's enough."

It's more than enough, it's essential, says Knocks, even for a hermit:

"If there's no close connection to anyone but yourself, there's a deficiency in you. I lived half a life before I realized it was more than a do-it-yourself job."

"It is the purest way to live."

That's William Carrington's take on being alone six months out of the year. "In essence, all of us *are* alone," says the retired New York advertising–PR executive.

"Being alone is inevitable," adds Carrington, sixty-five.

"Friendships change, friends leave. Children grow up, marry, and leave. People move from one part of the country to another, leaving close friends behind and making new ones. Passions cool, so lovers walk away from each other. The vow 'to cherish and to hold as long as you both shall live' is broken regularly, even by those who were certain their lives together would 'last forever.'

"Even in the best, most loving, most fulfilling, most passionate relationships, one or the other can be snatched away in the blink of an eye through accident or illness. So we are all, in the final analysis, on our own. That's a lesson I've learned, but it took a failed marriage, two or three failed relationships after that, plus a year and a half of hard work with a good therapist for me to come to the realization."

Carrington went on to marry, father three children, and rise to the position of vice president with a large Pacific Northwest bank, a career path that eventually led him to Chicago and then New York, where he formed his own highly successful public relations–marketing communications firm, taking on "highly exciting and challenging" product-promotion work for multinational firms such as IBM, American Express, and Bristol-Meyers, before he relinquished his Manhattan apartment two years ago to withdraw to Cape Cod.

Divorced in 1975, neither he nor his former wife have remarried. They remain good friends, he says, spending holidays and celebrations together with their children and grandchildren. Carrington's present relationship involves a companion seventeen years younger. His partner's buying trips for the art gallery he owns often take him away from home for long periods. Carrington freely indulges his own penchant for travel, particularly to South Florida, where he enjoys spending the winter months. The result is that they're apart as often as they're together, which suits them both fine.

"I've lived," says Carrington, "through too many northeastern and New England winters—scraping snow and ice off the car, digging out after blizzards, encasing myself in sweaters, coats, scarves, hats, gloves, and boots just to go the post office. Now, I love being able to get up in the morning, to throw on a T-shirt and a pair of shorts, and go for my morning walk in warm sunshine—in January, February, and March!"

As a result, Carrington figures, he and his companion spend approximately half the year together at their Cape Cod home. "I have more than enough solitude," he says, "and I love it."

Asked why, he replies. "For many years, I tried to find 'myself' while validating my worth through others. What a slippery slope that was! I also tried to change others into what I wanted them to be, rather than accepting our differences, and letting the little things go. I found you can't change anyone. Nor do most of us really want to. The only thing we can control, I finally found, is our attitude toward those differences—and dealing with the challenges they present, particularly in a close relationship or friendship. The focus needs to be on *self*, on the concept of 'being single.' In my opinion, this is key to our happiness with others."

"I need to say that being alone must be glorious because I have a husband who loves it," Helen Adams remarks, then prefaces her story with a plea: "Please note in your book that not everyone is afraid of being alone. Many choose this life from the onset, not wanting the responsibility or the sharing that is sometimes not easy. I only wish he'd realized the love he had for his life before he jumped into ours, making us feel like intruders. My husband lived alone for many years," Adams, thirty-four, relates.

"Then, at the age of thirty-seven, he decided to take on a widow and her two small girls. Well, he's never really given up his fondness for living alone, which makes life pretty miserable for the three of us who were looking for someone to share our lives with."

From the age of eleven, he had lived alone with his mother following their separation from an abusive father, Adams reveals. "Although there were four other siblings, they were all years older and out of the house by then. His mother worked and he found himself alone most of the time. We lived in a small town, and I knew him from high school. He was always very nice, but a bit of a loner. He sought me out after I became a widow, telling me he'd always loved me from a distance. 'Jackpot!' I thought, because he's actually quite wonderful. But he doesn't know how to be part of a couple or a family. He's tried," Adams concedes.

"But he lacks the skills because he's never been exposed to how a family should act. I really believe a person who has been with others and is suddenly left alone is in a much better position than a person who's been alone all along. If you've been with others and are suddenly alone, there's finally time to explore yourself—something you may never have had the chance to do. The freedom to do what you want and be what you want must be exhilarating when you're in the right frame of mind for it.

"On the other hand, people who've never had to share their space or time with others can be very dysfunctional, and not only lonely but self-centered. Sadly, they may not even realize their problem, because they've never known any other way to be.

"You see this with confirmed bachelors and women who've never married. There comes a point when they feel annoyance coupled with anxiety whenever they have to include others in their lives. My husband would deny this behavior in himself to the end. He'd say I was incorrect in my feelings, that ours is a normal marriage and family. I think he likes the convenience of having us when he needs us, but we have to realize when to go away whenever he has to revert to his world of aloneness. The way he pulls the rug out from under our feet—just when we think he's finally 'getting' it. It's crushing," she adds dejectedly.

"I'm not complaining, because I've decided to stay and live my life this way. One thing I've learned from the experience is how to be alone myself. He's taught me to depend on myself, and if I'm ever put in the position of having to do so, I'll be well-equipped. But I'm sure there's been heartbreak for many a wife, husband, and child put in the same situation."

"Men are extremely high-maintenance relationships," says Jean Culligan, fifty. "It takes constant work to keep one going, and I'd rather put my energy into something else right now. I'm healthy and happy on my own."

Neither of her two marriages were "any good," reveals the attractive motivational consultant who has been single for the past five years. Her first marriage, which lasted less than two years, ended when she was twenty-four.

"It was so brief it was inconsequential," Culligan dismisses the union. "He was wrong for me."

Married again when she was twenty-nine, her second husband had "significant problems with attachment," she says. "It took me way too many years to realize what was happening. I thought I could change him."

She presently lives with her six-year-old grandson, the child of her only daughter. "She's severely abusing drugs," Culligan reveals, "and I'm trying to decide whether or not to fight for custody of the boy."

That's the "something else" she's putting her energy into right now—and why she's content not to have anyone else in her life.

"Happiness is an 'I' thing," Culligan says. "It's *within* yourself. Nothing external is going to make you happy. Most women my age have spent a lot of time walking through pain to get to where we're OK with ourselves. Men don't do that. They're always looking for someone else to take care of them, particularly younger women.

"And I've come to a point where I don't want to take care of anyone—or have anyone take care of me. If I'm going to be with a man again, it will be strictly a give-and-take arrangement—and that doesn't have to involve marriage." Culligan's turmoil becomes evident as she talks about the emotional parameters she has set for herself.

"The person I'm going with now has teenage sons, and I'm at a point in my life where I don't want to live with any new humans. I want to say, 'You deal with *your* family, I'll deal with *mine*. You go back to *your* family, I'll go back to *mine*.' I've worked hard to get to this level of my life, and I can't lose control of it now.

"I've had tremendous issues to contend with, particularly in regard to my daughter. The effort has taken its toll. I have no energy left to give. If I'm going to commit to someone physically, emotionally, and spiritually, he has to know and accept that I'm an independent spirit, that I need my separateness."

"I can't be smothered. And I don't want a partner who wants to be smothered in return. If I have another relationship, it will combine togetherness and independence, freedom and dependency." Since becoming single, her best vacations have been with other women, Culligan reveals. "I think it's because there are no romantic expectations involved, and we can each do our own thing."

Also, her struggle with codependency has helped her develop the ability to fight for her personal as well as business needs, to tell others, "Hey, back off!" She can raise the roof if she has to, pull down walls, she says, quoting Katherine Hepburn to drive home her point: "If you obey all the rules, you miss all the fun."

Raised as a Roman Catholic, Culligan grew up work-oriented. "It was always work before play, work and *then* play. I had to be a rock. I tried to be *everybody's* rock. And I'm tired. Tired of being responsible, tired of taking care of others, tired of being 'no fun,' tired of buying toys for men and none for myself. Now I want to play. When I'm by myself I *can* play," Culligan says.

"When I'm by myself, I can *be* myself, which is what I want to be. Not just a part of someone else."

Approaching the eighteenth anniversary of a union she and her partner, Michael, have chosen *not* to consummate with a traditional marriage, Denise Scott asks with a grin, "If it ain't broke, why fix it?"

The fifty-two-year-old loan executive then adds seriously: "One reason I think it works is that we came to our relationship with family and friends whom each of us has allowed the other to remain close to—with or without the other. Neither of us would dream of telling one another, explicitly or implicitly, that we want any of those earlier ties severed," adds Scott, who was married for eleven years before starting her successful, long-term partnership with Michael, fifty-three.

"Each of us honors and respects the other's feelings for other people. Regardless of whether or not we share those feelings, we acknowledge their importance to each other. It means we sometimes take vacations apart," she says.

"Or we have separate dinners with friends. And that's perfectly all right with both of us. In fact, I think it's one of the most nurturing aspects of our relationship." There's another reason she's quite comfortable with her unorthodox partnership, Scott reveals.

"I watched my mother struggle to support the two kids still living at home when my dad left her after twenty-four years of marriage. She'd been a stay-at-home mom all that time and had never worked. So, even though she had some college education, her lack of job skills made her a less-than-attractive candidate for employment. I vowed I'd never be in that position. I always knew I'd support myself and work outside of the home, even when I had a family.

"As it turns out, I didn't have children. But I've always paid my own way—and I always will. It's been a bit of an obsession with me, I know, but I think it's one of the reasons Michael and I have very few strains in our relationship—financial or otherwise."

Alexis Padfield believes in tribes.

"Living alone feeds narcissism, creativity, and personal expansion," is how she explains her proclivity for communal living, "while relationships contribute to emotional growth, so I combine the best of both lifestyles."

The day we talked about her concept of tribal living, Padfield, sixty-one, had just returned from spending a month in Italy. Describing herself as "a Northwest-born-and-bred Libra, presently single, and *loving* it," she was married at the age of nineteen, divorced when she was thirty-three, remarried at fifty-one, and widowed at fifty-seven.

"Vastly experienced" at being alone, Padfield has trekked solo in Nepal, India, and Pakistan, hiked in France, Italy, and Switzerland, learned Italian, and lived for three months in Siena. And though she enjoys cycling, walking, kayaking, reading, attending concerts, movies, and the theater, entertaining friends has always been at the top of her list, she claims.

When she divorced in her early thirties, she embarked on a solo journey for the first time, Padfield says.

"I expanded my world by discovering what I personally enjoyed without parroting or being discounted by my husband. To my delight, my opinions were actually sought, and I enjoyed expressing them. I discovered a passion for classical music, the theater, and opera, none of which were a part of my growing-up or married years.

"Alone, I soon found an unfolding taking place as I soared toward my potential for living fully, and friendships were the wealth of my existence. As I became more interesting, so became my friends."

One day, she relates, a friend asked her to share their living arrangements. She agreed and wound up renting Portland, Oregon's, landmark Villa Marconi, an elegant house on the edge of a sprawling park. Padfield found a third roommate to share the monthly rent of $1,200—pricey back then. And there they were, she says, three women living together as self-proclaimed *Contessas*, complete with dime-store tiaras.

"We flew the Italian banner and held Sunday afternoon *suppa e vino e converzacione* for friends in front of the fireplace. The villa became the safe haven for our alter egos. Whenever invited to other social gatherings, the Contessas wore tacky 1950 net formals with their trademark tiaras.

"New friends assumed various Italian poses and became habitués of the exotic premises, including a strolling violinist and a resident wine steward, who dropped off cases of Bibi Caffe, which became our house drink. Our joy of life was infectious. But, alas, the villa was sold by the absentee owner and the Contessas had to pack up their tiaras and depart."

By then, however, the villa's fame had spread and another landlord sought out her acquaintance. "For years," Padfield relates, "this gentleman had rented out rooms in his graceful seven-bedroom home, but it was little more than a boardinghouse. He invited me to inject the same *joie de vivre* into his household. My first request was that he start over with a fresh crop of tenants. I suggested a male friend with a sailboat who loved to cook along with a woman whose avocation was also cuisine. We then advertised for a third woman whose energy and élan matched mine."

Their landlord's first love was fine wines, Padfield recounts. "The first of each month he would return home with four bottles, each of which he kept hidden in a paper bag, and poured samples of the household's potential 'vino of the month.' Each of us would vote our preference and the winning vintage became our 'house wine' for the next four weeks. We brought in guest musicians to entertain invited friends. Evenings were scheduled for 'experts' on intellectual subjects to enlighten us and generate discussions. Large sit-down dinners, hosted and prepared by 'tribal' members, became the norm."

Sailing in the San Juans and exploring the Northwest became part of their outdoor-oriented lifestyle. "Tribal living is not only stimulating but filled with camaraderie, since companionship is so readily available," Padfield points out. "Opportunities abound for both impulsive and planned joint activities, such as hiking, camping, exploring, walking, and overnight excursions to the beach and the mountains."

But then she married and moved to the suburbs.

When her husband was stricken with pancreatic cancer, they had been together only six years. "Knowing my enjoyment of others was a critical element of my joy in life," Padfield says, "he expressed his hope I would fall in love and marry again. I told him I didn't envision that for myself—not as a reflection on our marriage but because of my inclination toward narcissistic living."

"After his death I was a robot without emotions for eighteen months. I went on automatic pilot, keenly aware of two things. The first was the impact that turning over my sense of security had had on me. The second was the resurgent need to expand my own energy field, to empower myself fully once more. I couldn't shake the morbid thought of simply existing and then dying. I felt the renewed urgency to *live* while I could."

> "Tribal living is not only stimulating but filled with camaraderie, since companionship is so readily available."

Padfield gave her employer three months notice, sold her large house in the city, then relocated to a tiny coastal community 170 miles away. "Without knowing a soul," she says. "I set off for the unknown, feeling isolated and lonely at first. But after six months in my new home on the water, I went for a hike on a beautiful summer morning and felt the joy stirring in me once more at the sight of wildflowers blooming along the trail. This newborn happiness expanded with my growing awareness that I had to live in the present, in the *moment*. Healing journeys, I learned, take time. But while one looks back, one has to keep moving forward."

"Eventually, too, one has to stop looking back and look straight ahead. That's what I started to do once more. My solitary time in my new community brought a freshness back to my life. Living alone has blossomed into new self-discovery. My creativity manifests itself once more in gardening, journaling, meditation, in the renewed appreciation of daily life, in the capacity to enjoy each day, in the childish delight a rainbow, the full moon, and bird songs always bring."

And she began building a new tribe.

"Once again," Padfield reveals, "there's the spontaneity of shared experiences. We bring in guest musicians for indoor gatherings during the winter and for garden parties during the summer. We hold movie nights—rent videos and watch them with popcorn and soft drinks as if we were at a cinema. Again, there are the Italian dinner parties, wine tastings, bonfire music fests. For us, any excuse to gather is a good one."

There's even a tribal vehicle, she says. "Five of us got together and bought a 1983 Chevrolet half-ton pickup truck for $2,000. We each have our own key and an assigned day of use. We've named it 'Sweet Georgia Brown' because of its paint job. We keep it at a designated location. It's available for rental by friends for $25 a day, and the money goes into our maintenance pool."

Chapter Eight

The Tao of Now: Passion
for Each Passing Moment

*We are making hay when we
should be making whoopee; we
are raising tomatoes when we
should be raising Cain, or Lazarus.*
—ANNIE DILLARD

"Americans are funny," remarked Terence O'Donnell in a conversation we had about our national need to own as much as possible, including our joy. "We look for a *state* of happiness," said O'Donnell. "But the French know that's ridiculous. They accept that there are only *les petits bonheurs*, the little happinesses, only the moments: a sudden view, awakening to a superb morning, the sun's warmth, a cooling breeze."

Remember, counsels Zen master Thich Nhat Hanh, that *this* moment is the only time over which you have dominion. The most important thing in your life, therefore, is the thing you are doing at the moment. The most important person in your life is the person you are with at the moment.

And if you're alone, it follows, you must minister wholly and lovingly to yourself.

Mindfulness, Hanh calls it: an acute, constant awareness of everything we do, whether the act be grand, routine, or inconsequential—each moment we are doing it.

"When you are washing the dishes," he counsels, "washing the dishes must be the most important thing in your life. Just as when you are drinking tea, drinking tea must be the most important thing in your life."

Make each act, every movement a rite, a ceremony so vital as to be performed with a life-and-death awareness, Hanh instructs.

"Drink your tea slowly and reverently, as if it is the axis on which the whole world revolves—slowly, evenly, without rushing toward the future. Live the actual moment. Only this actual moment is life."

"When I lost my wife and then my job, when my three children were grown and had settled into lives of their own, I woke up one morning faced with ... myself," writes Brian Frazier, sixty-two, a retired newspaper editor, about his life alone.

"With that stark confrontation came the realization my existence had been so circumscribed by work and schedules, by career goals and family demands that my inner life had long ago disappeared. And so, with no alternatives or distractions to deter me, I focused on the one thing I had left: *today.*

"My only reminder of time passing became the beat of my heart, the changing seasons, the cycle of night and day. Gradually, I let go of all expectations, got in step with all that was happening to me *now.*

"I got up at five every morning to see sunrises I'd never seen before. I welcomed rain or sun or snow as what was needed *now*, content for each day to reveal itself—not as I had planned but with endless possibilities of its own.

"Awakening to my senses, I emerged from old dreams and strategems into 'born again' feelings long buried, grateful they had been with me all along, awaiting expression. I now plant roses with the sureness that what I nurture today will be here tomorrow, with or without me. A second chance? No. Rather, I think, a return to newness. It took a while, most of my life, but here I am finally attuned to the moment. Is this all there is? Maybe yes, maybe no, but this is now.

"This is *it.*"

Time is not something we can hang on to, David Steindl-Rast reminds us. "It is a gift we receive moment by moment."

Whatever you are doing, therefore, whatever you are thinking, whatever you are feeling becomes of crucial importance at that moment, says the Benedictine monk.

Wherever you are standing becomes holy ground. When you stand at the kitchen stove, the stove becomes your altar. When you lie on the bed, the bed becomes your altar, says Steindl-Rast.

"The whole monastic environment is explicitly geared to mindfulness. All the bells, gongs, and drums in a monastery are there to remind us: This is the moment, this is the moment."

Now now now now now. This is mindfulness, this is its mantra.

Jane Hamlin describes herself as a sixty-nine-year-old former child advocate and, in today's rueful jargon, a "displaced homemaker." But also a philosopher, and a poet, she adds.

She's a philosopher, Hamlin says, because from earliest memory she has wanted to know: "Why? How? What's happening?" And she is a poet, she says, because she has always felt the need "to find words for unspeakable feelings."

She remembers her younger brother, Johnny, telling her comfortingly, "You are not the average all-American girl." But she also recalls, more achingly, in the sixth grade all the other girls on the playground chanting, "S.C.! S.C.!"—meaning "Solitary Confinement!"—in their refusal to include her.

"Am I ugly?" she remembers asking herself. "I had freckles, wore glasses and orthopedic shoes. But I know now it was my *sadness* that drove them away."

Hurt deeply by having an absent father, a clinically depressed mother, and an abusive uncle—much more deeply than she would realize for a very long time—"like similar lost people, I never had a childhood," Hamlin relates. "I was a little adult and an uncomfortable older adult. The world was not as it should be if good will prevailed."

"Having little structure at home, I found a haven in school where I thrived on its predictability. Asking questions and *learning* was valued, and there always seemed to be answers. But in social situations, I was a misfit, often becoming confused and speechless.

"In college, I chose a major in sociology, a minor in philsophy, but took every English literature and writing course I could cram in, not conscious at the time that this was what my creative self really craved.

"Aside from skating and dancing, which I sensed were in tune with my deepest inner rhythms, and soccer—the only team sport I ever loved, not for the winning but for the running—I never learned to just *play*.

"But I did learn well how to *wait*. Waiting became my mode—*someday*, I told myself. If I stayed safe, took few risks, said and did little that might be criticized, if I had no rough edges, others could slip by me. I would become invisible, unthreatening, 'nice.'

"Of course, waiting became tantamount to collaboration with the enemy—my hidden self. Though my heart often trembled, I wore a mask of calm.

"I married late, infinitely tired, and for all the wrong reasons. I loved his hands and his smile, wanted to be touched, but did not know how to touch. I got what I paid for—no rewards except for three beautiful children, part of my longing, however undeserved. Still, they were easy to love, and I felt reverent toward them. I thought I could be a better mother than I had been a wife.

"When we moved for the fifth time in as many years to a house with a magnificent view but in another strange city, three thousand miles away from everyone I loved, I wrote a poem:

If you find me not within these walls,
look out upon the hills.
I have encircled me only from necessity...
My heart is in the highlands,
riding with the wind.
I fill my eyes with salmon dawn and silver eve,
Wanting to believe I am not bound
by this surround...
My soul is o'er the valley,
resting on the wind.

"This was self-acknowledgment," Hamlin says, "clearly a time to fly, but my wings were rusty, and I fell instead into the escape hole of drinking too much wine, to oblivion. Shadow Woman, a peak in Wyoming—*me*. Obscured by clouds of my own making, I hid from my beloved children as well—until confronted. From addiction therapy, I dared venture back to the field in which I'd earned my master's in social work—counseling others. But this newly self-assertive me was no one my husband recognized or wanted to see. The struggle had taken its toll. I had *waited* too long. When he left, I heard *clang* again, as in a recurring nightmare, the iron bars of 'solitary confinement.'"

"With my children grown and happily away, when I subsequently lost my job in a federally sponsored pilot program whose funds had run out, and at age sixty-four seemed obsolete, I lost the final bolster of feeling 'useful.'

"In a turbulent river, could I find a quieter place downstream to swim ashore? Whom to love? Whom to touch? Could I just finally *be*? There was still a feast before me—was I to be kept from it like the gluttons of Dante's *Inferno*, my hands chained?

"Could I see I wasn't bound—unless in a cage of my own imagining? Could I, who had always sought permission, free myself, give *myself* permission at last—to eat what and when I wanted, to sleep whenever I chose, to read endlessly, to play, to go back, if need be, to recover my lost childhood?

"I still have a passion for investing in children, to see that they're encouraged from early on to believe in themselves, to say—in *time*—what they need to hear of their uniqueness, to abet their respect for others, but, even more, to value themselves, to step-by-step become *human* beings in the best sense of the word.

"Can I do this for *myself* as well?

"With my grandson, I am revisiting childhood awe, rediscovering sing-song rhymes, pretending not to understand Monopoly so he can 'explain' it to me, reading fairy tales as if I've never heard them before, and 'oohing and aahing' as we watch *Pinocchio*. I am completely captivated by him. He brings me 'gifts'—pine cones, shiny stones that have caught his eye, and one day even a dead and bloody duckling! He is truly *present*. We *touch*.

"Even without his company, I am delighted at sensuous awakenings. Sometimes I buy myself shrimp, a 'sinful' self-indulgence, sometimes giant Hershey almond bars! I shuffle through autumn leaves, pick them up and give them to myself, just for their unique shapes and colors, as I used to bring them home, a bouquet for my mother. Having no one else to call on, I happily hammer and nail. I change light bulbs with serene confidence.

"I follow my heart, not my head—my feelings, not my thoughts. I am drawn to the simplest pleasures—geese winging across the changing sky, raindrops on roses, the sound of my children's voices. I melt with the snow and play with frisking dogs.

"I look into each passing face and accept others for who and where they are in time, not needing them to accept me—though with an old stubbornness, I must confess, I still look for those who seem to have an inner life.

"How far have I traveled in this new direction? I no longer count the years. I've been told I don't look my age, but that's because I've 'never lived in my face' before—the Irish in me, I excuse myself.

"But my soul is as old and as new as the millennium. This year I am two thousand years old, celebrating all I know of this time-span—*space* and *time* I've learned from Einstein. I welcome that space is my new marker—though not cyberspace, an enigma to me.

"I welcome silence from the voice that used to cry *wait*. I start each day searching the sky for all its portent. I light candles and simmer cinnamon sticks on the stove. I listen to my cherished classical records and to the Beatles, turned up as loud as I please, not just because I am, indeed, getting a little deaf, but to let the music possess me—take me all the way to Porphyry's spheres. I am comfortable with mystery. I postulate that if God is, hopefully, not a huge computer, then I'm sure He's a great musician!

"I write poems to what I see and love. I write down for my children all that touches me. And I've given up planning. Today, I think, I'll just *be* . . . a tree, if I like.

"I'll pretend I'm the first person in the world, besides Kilmer, to discover the wonder of trees. Today, I'll identify with that lonesome pine. I'll hold up my piece of sky, seek the sun, turn to the light, draw sustenance from a land that seems barren but has given me life.

"I'll testify to persistence and offer my frugal shelter if there be those who need it. If none, then I will stand alone. My roots are deep; I am firmly grounded; I may bend in the wind, but I will not fall.

"I will, of course, someday be gone. I will die, but then I hope my loved ones will honor the place where I once stood, their landscape now, and be comforted that I have finally found all that I sought—acceptance and peace. Perhaps my oldest son will remember that I once bought him a T-shirt inscribed, 'Be patient with me. God isn't finished with me yet.'

"I wear that T-shirt now."

Seeing, hearing, touching, feeling *only* the moment. Because we can only possess one moment at a time, and so only this moment counts.

An old woman asked Buddha how to meditate, relates meditation master Sogyal Rinpoche, author of *The Tibetan Book of Living and Dying*. "He told her to remain aware of every movement of her hands as she drew the water from the well, knowing that if she did, she would soon find herself in that state of alert and spacious calm that is meditation."

In the 1991 movie *City Slickers*, Jack Palance gives Billy Crystal profoundly simple advice. When Crystal asks him the secret of life, Palance holds up a forefinger, answers with a single word: "One."

Choose one thing. Do it to the best of your ability. Let it go. Pick something else. Repeat endlessly.

"I don't listen to music while I read," my friend Alberto Terego once told me. "I do one or the other, whichever I care more about doing most at the moment. Whatever I choose, I do it exclusively. If I'm going to read, I *read*. If I'm going to listen to music, I *listen*. Always in full participation of what the moment brings—whatever the moment, whatever the thing."

Forget about good time management when you're listening to music, urges survival psychologist Al Siebert. "Forget about being productive, about planning your day, shining your shoes, writing a letter, or cleaning out your desk. Just listen. Lean back and lose yourself in the music. The very word stems from the act of musing. Do it. Muse."

I try.

When I walk the beach, I consciously savor each step I'm taking, the softness of the sand, the warmth of the sun, the brightness of the sky, the rhythm of the surf. Now now now now now.

So much of life is spent looking back over our shoulders or gazing far ahead instead of wringing full benefit from the only thing we truly own: the moment at hand. How tragic not to fulfill its unique promise before it passes from us forever.

How much of our regret comes from wasting so many of our moments wanting something better, something different, something other than what we have at the moment that we have it?

Helen Ng practices mindfulness by pretending that everything she does she is doing for the very last time.

> "How many people allow their precious moments to pass because they think they'll have others just like them? Too many of those moments don't ever come again—and they are the stuff regrets are made of."

"I tell myself as I'm talking to someone that this is the last time I'll see or hear or speak to that person again," says the forty-six-year-old pharmacist.

"Or this is the last time I'll be visiting this place or experiencing this particular pleasure. This is the last chance I'll have to do whatever I need to do. Or say whatever I need to say. I remind myself that when this time passes, when this person leaves, when this chance is gone, it will never come again."

It's her way, she says, of not collecting any more regrets. "By thinking to myself this opportunity may be the last, I won't wait until it's too late."

For what? "For whatever," she replies. "To say thank you. Or 'You did a good job.' Or 'You were right and I was wrong.' Or 'I'm sorry.' Or 'I love you.' Whatever."

Pretending that each act, each event, each encounter, each occurrence could be the last makes *nothing* too trivial to put off, Ng says.

"How many people," she asks with a sad smile, "allow their precious moments to pass because they think they'll have others just like them? Too many of those moments don't ever come again—and they are the stuff regrets are made of."

Listening to Ng, I sense some of those lost moments were hers, and brought her to where she is today.

"Hold every moment sacred," exhorts Thomas Mann. "Give each clarity and meaning, each the weight of thine awareness, each its true and due fulfillment."

Stephen Levine, author of *Who Dies?* and *One Year to Live*, refers to mindfulness by another name: *impermanence*. Levine's doctrine of "conscious living and conscious dying" advocates a constant acknowledgment of life's transience, "in order to stay in the loving present, to live a life that focuses on each precious moment."

A constant acknowledgment of the ephemerality of life is the key to life itself.

We must accept, even welcome *all* change in order to live well and die well, affirms Sogyal Rinpoche. A deliberate awareness of "the continuing dance of birth and death, a dance of change," keeps us in the precious moment, says Rinpoche.

It's when we believe anything in life to be permanent, when we try to keep things the way we want them, that we shut off the possibility of learning how to live and how to die, he asserts. When we cling to permanence, when we struggle to thwart change rather than simply accept it, we become closed, we become grasping.

"It's the source of all our problems," claims the Buddhist meditation master. "Since impermanence spells anguish to us, we grasp onto things desperately, even though all things change. We are terrified of letting go, terrified, in fact, of living at all, since learning to live is learning to let go. This is the tragedy and the irony of our struggle to hold on. For not only is it impossible to do so, but it brings us the very pain we're seeking to avoid."

Personally, I wouldn't recommend the subject as a conversational gambit on first dates. In fact, no social occasion comes to mind where a discussion of our incredibly shrinking future would be greeted with much enthusiasm.

"So how do you feel about dying?" is a question best asked when we're alone.

But it's a dialogue we *must* initiate with ourselves eventually—the sooner the better, I truly believe. So does Ram Dass, who puts it this way: "Die in the morning so you don't have to die at night." I think what he means is that it's better to start preparing early than late.

Remember that old joke of the man who rushes out of the subway in New York City, grabs the first person he sees, asks breathlessly, "How do I get to Carnegie Hall?" And the guy answers, "Practice, man, *practice*."

Bad joke, good advice. Especially about dying.

"Most of us fight death as we fought life," claims Levine, "struggling for a foothold, for some control over the incessant flow of change that exemplifies this plane of existence."

Yet there is only one unchangeable law in the universe, points out Rinpoche, which is that *everything* changes. *All* things are transitory. Taking this doctrine of impermanence to heart, he says, softens our fear of loss and eventually frees us from our false passion for security and control—the shifting sands on which we attempt to build everything in our lives.

It's because of this desperate grasping for control, for permanence, that few of us die in wholeness, affirms Levine. Most of us live a life of partiality and confusion, thinking we actually own our bodies, he says.

"Few recognize it as just a temporarily rented domicile from which they must eventually be evicted. Those who see themselves as passengers in the body are more able to let it go lightly."

Our culture looks at life as a straight line, he says. The longer the line, the fuller the life, the less horrendous the end point. But in Native American culture, the wholeness of life isn't measured by duration but by the fullness into which one has entered into the passing moments. And by the acceptance of change as the simple, natural order of things.

By opening ourselves fully, then, to whatever each new moment brings—sorrow or joy, loss or gain, another beginning, another end, we open ourselves to the biggest moment of all: "Oops, what d'you know, there's death, how interesting...."

Chapter Nine

Sex and the Solitary Person:
Life Without Physical Intimacy

*If sex is so personal, why do we
have to share it with anyone?*
—ANONYMOUS

I feel like Ken Kesey's Nurse Ratched each time I say it, but my dog Buddy is much easier to live with since his operation, the one that makes men cross their legs in painful commiseration. He's still ninety pounds of rough-and-tumble Australian Shepherd, but the primordial drive to become Alpha Mutt has subsided along with his testosterone level. More mellow now, firmly in touch with his feminine side, he's discovered a universal truth women know instinctively and men seldom concede:

Life is simpler without sex.

That's the good news. The bad news: well, no sex.

But you're alone again, at least until the next Mr. or Ms. Wonderful comes along. Till then, I suppose, the thing to do is figure out what it was that sex with a partner provided you and see if you can create the same fireworks by yourself. Or a reasonable facsimile thereof. Or if you miss the pyrotechnics at all.

For sex, satisfactory or otherwise, has been deemed indispensable to human happiness since long before Freud ordained it a prime requisite of psychological health, which is why many therapists consider those who eschew it to be slightly off plumb.

What she misses most about being in a relationship isn't the sex, claims Alexis Padfield, sixty-one. "It's having a 'buddy' and the boyishness men never seem to lose. I miss having a pal to inspire me when I can't get myself up for that morning jog, lifting weights, or whatever's better done or more fun with a partner. I miss the spontaneous, available companion who's ready to run off to a movie at a moment's notice or haul out the kayak because the water looks great. I miss the teasing, the pranks, the male energy, and boyish humor."

Yet, it's been so long since she's had sex, she reveals, "I wonder if I'll ever feel passionately alive with sexual excitement again, whether I'll cross over that tremulous line into delirious desire once more. But the drive isn't nearly as demanding as it was when I was in my forties, therefore self-gratification has been fine."

A vibrator, Holly Hunter remarked in the movie *Copycat*, has become modern woman's "tool of survival."

"I still like to be with men," maintains Margaret Russo. But she makes it clear in exactly what ways: "I like one next to me in a movie. Or across from me at dinner. Or on a hike. I'd adore it if a man asked me to go ballroom dancing. But I don't miss having one in my bed."

She considers herself lucky to have a "stable" of good male friends for the occasional "man fix," adds Russo, sixty-six, but stresses again that she calls on them only for companionship. "When I've had a nice lunch or an enjoyable evening with a man, I feel renewed, spurred on, more alive. That's all I'm looking for. I haven't had a sexual interest in anyone for so long that I don't think I'd be bowled over again, not to the extent where I'd forfeit the joy I've found in being alone. Not to say the old machine isn't as lively as when I was a teenager," Russo points out.

"But it would take all the skills of a very unusual man to get me to share my body with him. I'm smart enough to realize that hooking up again would lead me back to dishpan hands, back to snoring, farting, and bad breath in bed. Not only would I be taking him on but his kids and grandkids. I'd be back to fretting over why he didn't mow the lawn, back to waiting an eternity for him to do something I could have done in five minutes. Worse, there would be my own resentful, deliberate tardiness in getting things done to *his* liking, to *his* satisfaction, to *his* specifications, and so forth and so on, ad marital nauseam."

"I'm also aware that most men—poor fools!—would prefer someone much younger than I," she continues. "By the same token, I don't intend ever again to be with anyone older. And if I did attract a man younger than myself, I'd suspect he was more interested in my purse than my physical charms."

"Yet I have women friends, some approaching my age, who openly admit to wanting a man to come along and sweep

> "I've replaced my sexual joy with the purely sensuous pleasures of working in my garden, wearing as little as the law allows so I can feel the sun on my skin."

them off their feet, to pay the bills. One of them is still placing and answering personal ads toward this self-delusional end."

So she's put her *Joy of Sex* books high on a shelf, says Russo. She's thrown her *How to Please Men* books in the garbage, and goes guiltless through her days, indulging herself in ways that have everything to do with sensuality and nothing to do with sex.

Married when she was nineteen and pregnant six weeks later, Russo was the mother of two sons and two daughters before she turned twenty-seven, had a hysterectomy when she was thirty-seven, and was divorced two years later. She is nurtured now, she says, by the twenty-one people she calls "family," including her eleven grandchildren and the ex-wives of her two divorced sons.

"My physical tensions can be relieved by bringing my trusty vibrator to bed," Russo readily admits. Or finding a good jet in the hot tub.

"But it isn't something I think much about anymore. I've replaced my sexual joy with the purely sensuous pleasures of working in my garden, wearing as little as the law allows so I can feel the sun on my skin."

"I inhale the scent of lavender and santolina, stir to the touch of branches and leaves caressing the insides of my arms and elbows, finding erogenous zones no man ever discovered.

"I drink quarts of water as I grow thirsty, feel my hair curl in the humid air, not caring whether twigs or mud perch within. I revel in the squish of mud between my toes as I work the soil barefooted, feel my muscles loosen, my skin grow hot and flushed and languid.

"My garden is my empty canvas, my yoga mat, my suntan booth, my weight room, and my marathon route. It's my soul restorer, my mud bath, my lover. In its earthy embrace, I plan my life—deciding what to pursue, what to ignore. It tests my memory, hones my fitness, enhances my endurance, strengthens my resolve.

"In my garden, I feel the sun on my face and lift my head to the sky in gratitude for the abundance of my life."

"Intimate attachments are a hub around which a person's life revolves, not necessarily the hub," says Anthony Storr, eloquent English aficionado of solitude. As important as sex is the development of an individual's capacity to be alone, "if the brain is to function at its best, and if the individual is to fulfill his highest potential," the acclaimed author of *The Art of Psychotherapy* and *The Essential Jung* points out in *Solitude: A Return to the Self*.

John Barrymore called sex that "thing that takes up the least amount of time and causes the most amount of trouble." Unsurprisingly, it was also Barrymore who described love as the "delightful interval between meeting a beautiful girl and discovering that she looks like a haddock."

Garrison Keillor offered another perspective: "Sex is good, but not as good as fresh sweet corn."

Alan King also placed food above sex—salami with eggs, to be exact. "Now that's better than sex," he once told Mimi Sheraton of *The New York Times*, "but only if the salami is thickly sliced."

For new hermits, though, sex becomes like a basket of onion rings—still tempting but happily forfeited now for reasons of gastric and psychic equanimity.

Still, make no mistake about sex being the omnipotent urge, the supreme itch, the compelling force. The ability to inspire lust remains the ultimate power, the ace card in the eternal poker game of the sexes, assuring us once again of life's three certainties: death, taxes, and cosmetic surgeons.

Conversely, those able to extricate themselves from its timeless thrall wield a power of their own: freedom from the self-imposed tyranny of sex.

Perhaps it's never too early to rely on other persuasive powers. As Salman Rushdie's supermodel girlfriend, Padma Lakshmi, told a newspaper reporter, "When people say things like: 'Oh, you're so beautiful,' I like to respond: 'Yes, and my brains don't sag, either.'"

In *The Road Less Traveled*, his classic primer on the psychology of love, M. Scott Peck does, indeed, liken the myth of romantic love to a form of sexual bondage. To be *in* love means to be sexually motivated, consciously or unconsciously, he says.

"Or to put it in another, rather crass way, falling in love is a trick that our genes pull on our otherwise perceptive mind to hoodwink or trap us into marriage."

W. Somerset Maugham said the same thing: "Love is only a dirty trick played on us to achieve the continuation of the species."

Without this sexual ploy of nature to keep the world populated, claims Dr. Peck, "many of us who are happily or unhappily married today would have retreated in wholehearted terror from the realism of the marriage vows."

In other words, without romantic—*lustful*—love to befuddle our minds and muddle our reasoning, the decision to remain single would be a simple one.

Now, if sex and solitude are equally important to you, perhaps you should consider the Hertz/Avis Plan: leasing with no intention of owning, visitation rights rather than full occupancy, having one's proverbial cake and eating it too.

While traditional unions assure regularity, dependability, and constancy, the latter option provides flexibility, variety, and independence.

Which are more important to you at this juncture of your life?

Another marriage, even another relationship, is the last thing on her mind right now, claims twice-divorced Angie Corcoran, who has been alone for the past fourteen months. She hasn't even dated in that time, reveals the fifty-year-old California real estate agent.

"All I can say is maybe one day. At this moment, all I want to do is to take care of myself. I don't want to think for someone else. I don't want to wash, iron, or clean for someone else. I don't want to cook if I don't feel like it. And if I want to go to bed early or late, I don't want to have to worry whether my husband's need for sex has been met for the week," Corcoran says.

"I know it sounds selfish," she adds, "and it probably is. But I've never had the opportunity to be selfish, and you know what? It's absolutely wonderful!"

Remember, now, that we're talking about sexual or "cathectic" love: the willful investment of one's psychic energy in another because of physical passion rather than the higher plane of True Love.

Partners who *love* each other, as opposed to being *in* love, Peck points out, nurture one another and their relationship in ways other than sexual. A characteristic of real love, he notes, is the distinction between oneself and one's partner that is deliberately maintained and preserved.

In the thrall of their physical passion, therefore, few people who are *in* love willingly distance themselves from the objects of their cathexis. Many who *love*, on the other hand, choose to be alone for a myriad of personal reasons, having nothing to do with sex and everything to do with "self" in the context of the *Webster's* definition: "the entire person of an individual."

Penelope Russianoff made it clear that she did not write *Why Do I Think I'm Nothing Without a Man?* for women who have no need of a man around the house—autonomous women capable of being alone, even of living alone and liking it. She wrote the book, she said, for those who need to find and develop their "selfhood," to feel good about themselves as people.

One of the best ways to achieve this, said Russianoff, is by "learning to love being alone." In a chapter by that title, she tells of a woman who always became depressed when watching a spectacular sunset alone because such an event, she felt, wasn't worthwhile without a lover to validate and enhance the experience.

But one evening, Russianoff reports, the woman became fascinated with the colors of the setting sun and, for some reason, focused only on what she was experiencing and how she felt—not on who was or wasn't there to experience the beautiful sight with her. "She let herself thrill to the experience, become involved with the experience. And it was a revelation."

What this woman had done, unconsciously, selflessly, says Russianoff, was to substitute sensuality—the gratification of her senses—for sexuality, which she had always associated with the romantic experience of watching a gorgeous sunset.

We limit ourselves severely when we buy into the belief that we need someone else to fulfill our sensual needs, similarly cautions Rae Andre, author of *Positive Solitude*.

Make sensuality rather than sexuality a goal, Rae suggests, for there are many intensely pleasurable moods that aren't sexual, moods attuned to *all* of our senses.

"Many people who are alone discover a heightened aesthetic sensuality," says Rae. "Freed from the preoccupation of organizing a household complicated by other lives, they can focus on making their living space an extension of themselves. They discover their own taste. They make a point of collecting art and other things that satisfy their aesthetic sense."

Make your home a sensual place in which to live, she encourages. Fill it with bright, fragrant, textured, highly tactile, emotionally evocative furniture, decorations, and objects. Create a wonderful physical and emotional environment to experience on a daily basis.

"It should come as no surprise that in these lovely environments, sensual people make love to themselves," adds Rae.

Still, the concept of self-pleasuring remains offensive to many Americans, as both Pee-Wee Herman and former surgeon general Joyce Elders learned to their dismay a few years ago. Herman, as you recall, was caught *in flagrante* in an "adult" movie house. And the highly competent Elders was fired by President Clinton for her suggestion that masturbation be discussed in the nation's classrooms as a safe method of sexual gratification.

"Not many of the best things in life are free, but by any sensible reckoning masturbation to climax is one of them," an editorial in *The Nation* later noted. "An amazement to the young, an aid to insomniacs, providing ease in an edgy world, it is, above all, a pure and unproductive pleasure."

And not just for kids anymore.

Oscar-nominated (*Titanic*) actress Gloria Stuart, who is ninety, reveals with alacrity in her autobiography, *I Just Kept Hoping*, that she doesn't need men anymore: "I had and have no guilt whatsoever when it comes to pleasuring myself."

"Don't knock masturbation," chides Woody Allen. "It's sex with someone I love."

Irish novelist and poet James Joyce praised its "amazing availability."

American writer Truman Capote liked not having to dress up for it.

Hollywood director Milos Forman appreciates not having to talk afterwards.

"It's taken me half a lifetime," marvels *Women on Top* author Nancy Friday, "and the writing of six books, all of which deal at least in part with sexuality, to appreciate the role masturbation plays in our lives. Here is the most natural thing in the world ... yet we feel guilty as thieves, our sense of self lessened when it should be heightened by mastery and self-love."

Pity, then, the Portnoys of the world, suffering the torments of the damned for their private, palliative acts. But what are the alternatives?

Well, there's always the Heidi Fleiss option—though an illegal, even fatal choice these perilous days. When the name of Hollywood actor Charlie Sheen cropped up on the Hollywood madam's client roster, many wondered *why*? When any number of women would gladly have accommodated him without monetary compensation?

A possible answer: some fear the complications of sex more than AIDS.

Then, of course, there's good old-fashioned celibacy. Among those who sing its ardent praises is Oblate priest William McNamara, who concedes that sex is, indeed, wonderful: "Nothing can take its place. A woman evokes from a man, and a man from a woman, something that is not otherwise invoked."

But what?

"I think it is important," McNamara remarks in his marvelous book, *Speaking of Silence*, "that we develop within the monastic tradition this idea of celibate lovers—that we learn how to be highly sexed, and to have warm, intimate, passionate relationships, and yet be willing to deliberately renounce the genital privileges and pleasures of spousal love. That is the religious celibate's expression of love."

Celibacy certainly carries the Vatican seal of approval. And monks through the ages have endorsed it highly, even though their enforced abstinence is reputed to have driven countless men from the priesthood while discouraging legions more from joining.

"But there are wonderful fruits and byproducts that come from that kind of free, deliberate renunciation," encourages Father McNamara. "Celibacy provides a particular freedom that is not otherwise achieved."

Then, again, it's not for everyone, particularly at an early age. As Saint Augustine allegedly prayed: "Lord, give me chastity—but not yet."

Perhaps the same goes for solitude.

Lusty SWF wants physically
intimate relationship, no
walks, beaches or dancing. I
am 44, slender and uninhibited.
You are a man, 25-50, attractive
to me and willing to exchange
photographs. No smokers,
women, couples, marrieds.

This ad ran in an alternative weekly newspaper of a northwestern city in the summer of 1996. Sharon Henley placed it in the "Other" section of the personals, she said, because she wasn't looking for the "usual" type of relationship.

She further stipulated her personal preferences in the ad's accompanying voice-mail recording, to make it absolutely crystal clear what kind of union she was looking for. "I included the kinds of looks and attitudes I liked, stuff such as 'clean-shaven, active liberal, green politics,' and gave similar info about myself: '5'2", brunette, healthy, a runner.' I made it clear I wasn't interested in a cozy, domestic relationship, but I did want a monogamous one."

Before placing her ad, Henley thought long and hard about exactly what she was after. "I wanted sex, period," she said emphatically. "I also wanted it to be with a man I respected and to whom I could be physically and romantically attracted."

"I saw in my mind's eye a loving relationship with a man who would be available to me once or twice every couple of weeks. He needed to be busy and involved in his own life and, again, someone I would find physically attractive."

"This necessitated the exchange of photos, therefore the rental of a post office box and the use of an assumed name." Henley explained why she chose the personals: "It would have been awkward approaching a man and saying, 'I think you're very sexy. Would you be interested in getting together a couple of times a month for a mutually satisfying slap-and-tickle?'"

"This way I could interview likely candidates and select a man with whom I shared common interests, feelings, and concerns, and a regard for the environment. I didn't want anyone who was too much into the money thing. All in all, if he wasn't exactly right for me, then I'd reject him outright. I didn't have the time or inclination to work on one damn thing about him."

She thought she'd get a "good" response, Henley said. "I had no idea 180 men and 3 women would reply!" Listening to her in fascination, I couldn't help smiling as I visualized them reading the ad—exulting, "Yes, there *is* a God!"

She tried to be kind with them, she said. "I explained to each person I talked to that I needed to contact everyone before I made a final decision. I narrowed the list down to three, met with them in person, and settled on a thirty-one-year-old grad student who works at a health food store."

Henley described him as "very funny, intellectual, and green." Another plus, Henley pointed out, was that he didn't own a car, which meant it would be difficult for him to "just show up" at her home in the rural area to which she had moved several months earlier.

"Anyway," Henley went on, "we've been seeing each other for about a month now. He rides his bike to a town halfway between the city and where

I live, and I pick him up and drive him the rest of the way to my place. That's our arrangement. I enjoy him. He calls me once or twice a week, which is just right. It's early yet, but so far, so good. I'm glad I did this. And I'm glad I chose him."

I asked her why she hadn't tried to meet a suitable man in the community to which she'd moved. "I'm still struggling with being the new single woman here," Henley replied.

"I'm finding that, though remote in location from populated areas, it's quite close in terms of social life. That has its benefits and detriments. On the one hand, it means that people want to be friends, and if I need help it's readily available. It also means that people think it's OK to just 'drop by.' I hate that! I have six freakin' acres and I can't walk around in a sports bra because someone's husband is always coming around to see how I'm 'doing.'"

"So far I've had three men come on to me. I suppose it would be all right if they were the right kind—and sometimes I feel guilty for being uninterested, that I should be grateful for their attention. But it's more than irritating to me, it's annoying," Henley continued.

"I try to be clear about not wanting a relationship. I'm alone, I tell them, because that's what I chose, what I enjoy. Then they pretend that all they're interested in is my friendship. Do they think I was born yesterday?"

"There was a man who installed a bathtub and water heater in my house when I first moved in. It took him six weeks! And he spent half that time making sexual innuendos. I finally had to tell him bluntly I wasn't interested. I'm sure that when the people checking me out find I really feel that way, they'll leave me alone," she said, her exasperation loud and evident.

"Why do men think women can't do without them?"

Chapter Ten

A Logo for Those Alone:
No Fear! And No More Regrets

No human being ever,
in the end, outran regret.
—THOMAS H. COOK

Last night, I dreamt I played soccer again. I was twenty once more, a freshman at the University of San Francisco in that glorious fall of 1954, running
and leaping effortlessly, gliding across soft green grass with young legs,
young lungs, the boundless vigor of my youth. It was the last time I ever
played soccer.

I woke from my dream with such a deep sense of loss that I never want to
experience the feeling again. But I know I will. Of all my remembrances, I
dwell most on that last year of carefree play under denim skies in a city of
bridges by a pewter bay. The memories return with such longing that they literally take my breath away.

But I understand the searing nostalgia the halcyon images always trigger,
for my longing has to do with one of the most profound regrets of my life: a
decision not to return to my field of dreams despite the college scholarship
that would have remained mine until I graduated.

There were three All-Americans on the team on which I became a starter
in my freshman year. Having grown up playing soccer in the Philippines, I
excelled at the sport, which was still in its infancy in the United States.
Another 1954 freshman at the University of San Francisco with the same ath-
letic scholarship was Bill Russell. Unlike me, he returned to lead the school
to two NCAA basketball championships, then went on to star for thirteen

seasons with the Boston Celtics, leading them to eleven NBA titles, eight of them in a row.

It wasn't just the game of soccer that I gave up—although I still wonder how good I could have become, and where the road from San Francisco might have taken me. My poignant regret is that I so nonchalantly ended my youth, blithely discarding those remaining seasons in the sun.

I dwell sometimes on a stanza from the poem "Summer Solstice" by George Seferis:

The blank page speaks with your voice,
your own voice,
not the one you like;
your music is this life
you wasted.
You could regain it if you wish,
if you fasten to this indifferent thing
which casts you back
there where you set out.

"Regrets?" she asks.

For Jane Hamlin, the family counselor, who at the age of fifty-four faced a life alone after a twenty-two-year marriage, this question did not seem unexpected. "Oh, yes, I'm sorry I couldn't have done a better job of loving my husband, as hard a man as he was to love," she replied.

"I'm glad that he still comes to visit me, that we share events with our children. Though he divorced me—I didn't divorce him—I still see him as someone who was given me to love. I think he needs me to care if he is happy or unhappy, if he lives or dies, and *I do—I care*. I need to know he's OK (and I *love* his dog!). But I haven't told him so.

"There are so many people I've not told so many things, whom I've not thanked for having appeared in my life, like guideposts, bearing their gifts of friendship. I was a 'difficult' friend, but so many were forgiving. I cover my ears from the bell that tolls: 'Too late! Too late!'

"I would liked to have told my mother in the words of that wonderful song from *The King and I*, 'You may not always do what I would have you do, but all at once you do ... something wonderful!'

"And I would have liked to have hugged my father, who once *almost* hugged me.

"I would like to have back my beloved friend Rita, who personified unconditional love, who loved me despite the warts, whom I called 'Slats' and who called me 'Sunshine'—*terms of endearment*, of which there are so few. I would like to say and hear those words again.

"My Aunt Emily ... who spent her whole life of ninety-five years in one small town not far from Richmond, Virginia, and near Appomattox: Amelia Courthouse, where the Civil War actually ended, they say, because it was there Lee's supply wagons were halted.

"Part of the history I have lost, my Aunt Emily—never have I known a loving spirit such as hers, so *giving* she still shines for me, a permanent lodestar in my life, although gone these last five years. If ever I could design a house for myself that seemed like hers, a haven, it would have white organdy curtains and beds high off the floor so that one needed a footstool to climb into them.

"It would have the sound of her footsteps, 'dot-and-carry' (from crippling arthritis, which nonetheless never crippled her soul), and the sweetness of her voice calling me, 'Sugar,' from the kitchen, swept and full of light, and the aroma of fried chicken. I wish I could have understood earlier that 'rooms without love are just rooms,' that it is not a *place* that makes memories but the people at its center, who *are* its center.

"I used to think I had invented the concept of 'centering' when I first felt the imbalance within me ... until I met Polly Peacock, an artist, with her potter's wheel.

"Friendless in a city new to me, huge and daunting Chicago, and even though I'd had my first beautiful child there, I felt completely lost ... until Polly. When we first met in a park at the foot of Addison Street bordering Lake Michigan, it was a cold, gray, snow-struck day, reflecting my inner state.

"Our one-year-old girls made an instant bridge between us, which, out of shyness, I feared to cross. But she, with her zest for life and unwavering warmth, reached out, and offered—*friendship*.

"Though I do not see her much anymore—thirty years have passed since then—it comforts me to this day to hear that she is still fully involved in life, a true *spirit*. Why have I never acknowledged this to her? I know she doesn't need it—but perhaps I need to say it: that she has such a meaningful place in my heart, though our lives have touched only briefly.

"I will always remember that when I told her of my sense of needing to return to my 'core,' she handed me a book on pottery called *Centering*. Intuitively she knew there were truths there, truths I had seen flowing from her heart to her mind's eye, to her hands, to her potter's wheel."

I know this now about regrets: they don't go away. Most things distance themselves with time and space, to eventually slide off the edge of our consciousness and disappear forever, but not regrets. You can shove them aside, disavow them for a lifetime, but they always return. And the longer you deny them, the more they punish you when they can no longer be held at bay.

Regrets are particularly poignant for the old and the dying, those who have used up most of the chances they'll ever get and are left to make peace with their failed choices. Regrets are why I've always thrilled to the closing lines of Charles Dickens's *A Christmas Carol*. It took being scared witless just in time, but old Ebeneezer was allowed to revisit his failed choices and make them right. The codger came through with flying colors, wiping out a lifetime of regrets, as Dickens recorded:

"Scrooge was better than his word. He did it all, and infinitely more.... He became as good a friend, as good a master, and as good a man, as the good old city knew, or any other good old city, town, or borough, in the good old world."

I remember what the dying man from Iowa told me on the Oregon coast. *We are the sum of our choices*. The right choices result in our goodness and character. The wrong choices harden into bitterness and despair. And if we don't have the wisdom to make good choices when we're young, we need the grace to make peace with the bad ones when we're old.

Luckiest of all are those who still have the time to replace their bad choices with good ones. Good choices in the nick of time can banish regrets.

"What is the biggest regret of my life?" Sharon, a forty-six-year-old nurse practitioner, asks herself. "As I ponder that question on this last Valentine's Day of the old millennium, I think it is that I chose to follow a path I *thought* would lead to fulfillment, rather than to continue along one that I knew had me well on my way," she answers herself.

"I should have pursued a higher vision for myself, studied hard, stayed single, and gone to medical school. Instead, I tried to balance what I thought was 'love and life.' I became involved with a guy who really wasn't good for me, and I became a bedside nurse. *Big* mistakes.

"There's nothing wrong with being a bedside nurse, but it wasn't right for me. I traded my intellectual curiosity and drive for a career that was only sort of what I really wanted, and a home with a man who believed my purpose, joy, and fulfillment was however he defined them. I eventually lost track of who I was.

"Eventually, there were three lovely children and I gave up nursing to be home with them. I adore my children; I did that willingly and I'll never regret giving life to them. But the man to whom I gave the best years of my life eventually met the love of *his* life, and I was history. I've been playing catch-up with my life ever since.

"I'm now back in school, pursuing pretty much what I should have in the first place. That's the great part. The not-so-great part is that, at this point in my life, I have so much less time, energy, and freedom to devote to launching a new career. My roles often conflict and I often feel that I don't quite do justice to any of them: mother, nurse practitioner, and student.

"The result is I often feel that, while I'm finally getting my own life back, I may never truly have the one I wanted. I guess the truth is that my life is what it is and I must strive to joyfully bloom where I've been planted.

"In my effort to spare my two wonderful daughters similar regrets, I try to model and to speak the truth about what love really is. I offer these truths to all girls and to the adults who love them:

"Parents, strive to know, to cherish, and to honor the unique individuals your daughters were created to be. Nourish the vision that they have for themselves. Model for your daughters healthy interpersonal boundaries, self-respect, and respect for *all* people as valuable individuals.

"Girls, absolutely honor your own vision for your life above anyone else's. Never honor another person's ridicule of you or your choices. As much as you can, do not impose limits on what you can do with your life; always 'go for it.' Finish your education before you settle down and absolutely *never* sacrifice your own identity or purpose for the 'love' of some guy.

"True love never demands that."

"Phil and I met when we were both ten years old," says Ruthie, sixty-five, a retired business manager. "I moved away when I was twelve, but our paths crossed again when we were fifteen. We dated all through high school and eloped six weeks after graduation. We had five great kids by the time we were twenty-four. At the age of twenty-six, we both fell in love with a big, old farmhouse and bought it. We had a good time raising the kids there. They all had horses, goats, chickens, pigs, llamas, donkeys, geese, ducks, dogs, cats, raccoons, cows, and even a pet snake. Then, as always happens, they grew, and one by one left for schools or for marriage and, once again, we found ourselves alone in our big, old house," she relates.

"Phil was an over-the-road truck driver and I would often go on trips with him. They were always fun. We also owned a 33' Richardson boat, and for six years Phil and I would live on the boat from the first of April to the middle of November. We loved it.

"On August 25, 1991, one day after my fifty-seventh birthday, Phil was diagnosed with a carcinoid tumor of the lower abdomen. He had bypass surgery and lived for two pain-and-misery-filled years. He was buried three days before my fifty-ninth birthday.

"Now, I'm still living in the big, old house that we both loved and regretting that I didn't do what he asked when he would say, 'Honey, why don't you leave that for tomorrow and come here and sit with me?' Why was it so important to me to do those dishes or dust that furniture instead of cuddling up to him in front of some dumb war movie or western on the TV?

"Today, I would give anything just to lay my head on his chest and feel his heart beating again, even for a minute. I used to tell him, 'I'll be there in a minute, Honey, just as soon as I finish this whatever.'

"Oh, God, how many minutes have I wasted?"

"When I was fifteen, my father died of AIDS," says Jen, twenty-three. "I've told myself, 'I'm glad I didn't say good-bye. He wouldn't have remembered me. He wouldn't have been himself or looked the same. I couldn't go on the rest of my life remembering him in that way.'"

"But now, as a mother, it's all so different. I wish I'd had that last good-bye. I wish I had told him how much I loved him, how much he meant to me. I'll always remember him holding out his hand to walk with me across the street or taking me to school or shopping in Seattle—all the little things we did together that now, as a woman, seem so much bigger."

Sharon's, Ruthie's, and Jen's regrets were given to me by Barry Cadish, a man exceedingly conversant with the subject. He has more than a few of his own, but he wants more—as many as he can get. He set up an Internet site to collect them and plans to fill a few books with the regrets that soon came pouring in. The first of them, *Damn! Reflections on Life's Biggest Regrets*, is now in print.

"Regrets are a good thing because of the wisdom and insights we can gain from them," Cadish told me at the Portland, Oregon television studio where he writes and produces public service announcements when he isn't trolling for regrets. "Reading a book filled with regrets may help people realize their own lives aren't that bad. Perhaps they won't take so much for granted," he said.

"Maybe they'll identify with one or more of the stories and make positive changes instead of continuing down the same old road."

Diane MacLean, sixty-four, remembers her father as the one person who showed her "what love truly is." His sacrifices for his children were endless, she recalls. "He never took up golf until we were grown and gone. He covered for my mother, who did a lot of napping while we were teenagers and spent many more hours smoking and drinking to make her dreary days pass quickly. His love never wavered—and he was strict!"

MacLean remembers him running out to rap on the car windows if her teenage date turned rapturous past her curfew.

"I knew he cared about me more than I cared about myself. Because of my Dad's love and the lack of it from my Mom, I became Supermom to my own children. I was going to be a far better role model for them than the one I'd been raised with, I swore. But I wore the costume and cape too long, trying to make my marriage work as well. My kids respected me for that, but it wasn't until many years later that I learned their father was mistreating as well as neglecting them. By then the resentments and regrets had begun to pile up. One of the biggest of them was that I hadn't finished college.

> "Regrets are a good thing because of the wisdom and insights we can gain from them."

"I'd been obsessed from the time I was five with the dream of going to college—to learn and achieve and grow. But I bought the sorry line, 'Why do you need an education when you have me?' I heard it and succumbed, but deep down I believed I'd have my degree someday.

"I told myself, 'You're going to invest your time in something no one can ever take away from you—an education.' And four kids and twenty-three years later, I had the diploma. I graduated with only half a credit more than I needed and didn't even feel the need to put on a cap and gown and go in for the ceremony. As soon as my diploma arrived in the mail, I felt triumphant. And the regrets and resentments went away.

"The next thing I did was go down to Nordstrom's with my credit card, as I'd existed for three years in my sons' cast-off jeans. I had the next phase of my life to attend to, something called *earning a living*."

Regrets are a constant visitor to the old man at the beach. They come and they go at all hours of the day and night. He lets them in, barring none their entry, allowing all their full measure of blame so that when they return the next time, and the next, they will be a little less hurtful.

By remembering, he thinks, he will understand. By understanding, he will be able to forgive—himself above all. And through forgiveness, the regrets will begin to resemble hope.

Chapter Eleven

Achieving Egolessness: Getting Out of Our Own Way

It is far more impressive when
others discover your good
qualities without your help.
—JUDITH MARTIN

"I, who worked hard at being special, fell in love with a people who value being ordinary."

These are the opening words of Sue Bender's remarkable book, *Plain and Simple*. In her eloquent tribute to the joys of unadornment and naturalness, the ex-New Yorker, artist, therapist, wife, and mother of two sons recounts her spiritual journey to "a landscape of immense inner quiet."

Absorbed into the timeless rhythms of two Amish families, she learned about simplicity, daily commitment, and the joy of "doing what you do well."

Before Bender's defining moment (in a men's clothing store where she was drawn to a display of old Amish quilts), which launched her on a journey to "a part of me I had ignored, even depreciated," her life had been "like a crazy quilt," a pattern she hated:

"Hundreds of scattered, unrelated, stimulating fragments, each going off in its own direction, creating a lot of frantic energy. There was no overall structure to hold the pieces together. The Crazy Quilt was a perfect metaphor for my life."

Bender's words struck home because my own life had been one of disconcerted intensity, driven by an irrational need to—what? Achieve, measure up, be worthy? Of whom? Of what? I was constantly riding off in all directions—and never getting anywhere.

In the summer of 1990, I impulsively left Portland to become the creative director and copy chief of a South Florida advertising–public relations agency. Soon afterwards, during a phone conversation with my daughter, she asked me what I did for a living in Miami. "I help the rich," I told her, "plat, parcel, and pave the land for the benefit of a privileged few."

Madeline laughed and dropped the subject. Had she persisted in her query, however, I would have explained that I earned my sizable income by helping residential-resort developers market and promote their pricey real estate in pristine portions of the country.

In these dwindling Edens of America, serenely distant from the blighted urban and industrial centers, luxurious gated communities with P. B. Dye golf courses, Har-Tru tennis courts, and plantation clubhouses are providing privileged sanctuary for prosperous expatriates fleeing the crowded metropolises from which they mined their fortunes. Here, buffered against common folk who lack the price of admission, surrounded by the finest social and recreational amenities money can buy, the equestrian classes are living out their gated dreams. For a time I excelled at marketing those dreams.

And I learned about massive egos.

I recall a business trip I made to Maui with several agency staffers. Our mission was to impress our finely honed skills on a prospective client who planned to convert a mountainside of sugarcane overlooking a cobalt bay into a panoply of residential estates and condominiums. For two agenda-crammed days and nights, high-powered panjandrums on all sides of the table raised the tropical humidity to oppressive levels with their grandiloquence and bombast.

I remember, midway through one of the interminable meetings, jotting on my note pad: "If ego were dynamite, we could blow up half this island."

That was my own defining moment. A few weeks later I resigned the highest-paying job I'll ever hold, packed a U-Haul truck, and drove back to Portland. When I reached the Columbia Gorge on the final leg of my journey home, I sidled to a stop at the river's edge and breathed my thanks to the vast blue sky above the sweet brown earth.

I still marvel at how I lasted eighteen months in a place so distant in temperament to the Pacific Northwest, but I am grateful for the lessons I learned there, particularly those having to do with ego.

The Art of Self, I've learned, is indispensable to material success but corrosive to the human spirit. What's more, much of the misery in the world, I've decided, is caused by people who take themselves too seriously. Certainly, most of the unhappiness I've brought on myself has come from trying to impress others.

The people I find most appealing nowadays are those so secure in who they are, so lacking in ego, pretense, and guile, that they can allow others simply to be themselves. It is, I think, the rarest of privileges: the freedom to be completely oneself in the company of others.

Unfortunately, though, it's a gift we have to give ourselves, for no one can make us feel what we don't want to feel.

"If you're immediately at ease with a creative idea, take another look. It's probably not an idea at all."

It's an old advertising maxim, says fifty-nine-year-old copywriter Merrilee Wheeler, and in it she recognized her daughter.

"What the maxim cautions," says Wheeler, "is that if you're immediately comfortable with an idea, it's because you've heard it, absorbed, accepted it, and it now has the ring of truth. If it scares you, however, take a second look. Although an advanced, energetic scholar, my lovely Alison evinced a trait—probably, alas, learned from me: self-doubt, the tendency to stand in her own shadow," she adds.

"This struck me particularly one day when, in her late twenties, she asked me, 'At my age, do you think I should be married?' I could only answer, 'Is there someone you'd *like* to marry? If not, then *no!*'

"I was afraid she was labeling herself, limiting who she was. Why? To match her peer group, to seek a *title* that would give her instant status? Was she facing challenges she felt she couldn't hurdle? In her fear of failing, was she seeking familiar answers—a *sure* way to failure?

"Her question triggered remembrance of a time earlier on when I had expressed heartfelt admiration for her seeming ability, even from childhood, to figure things out for herself. She had blurted words which still resonate: 'A little guidance would have helped, Mom!'

"Could I guide now? Had I learned anything worth passing on to encourage her on *her* way? Where was the 'ego' I had tried so hard to foster in her—'ego' as in her sense of self? Was I sure enough of *myself* to make up for a lack finally acknowledged?

"I could but try. I told her of a woman I hardly knew in a depression recovery group, who one day had startled us all with a sudden question: 'Why are we still struggling? *This is life!*'

"For myself, the answer came in a line from Michael Ondaatje's novel, *The English Patient*: 'When you meet someone who is still struggling, you postpone giving up!'

"To Alison, I offered, 'Accept that you won't always be able to predict an outcome, but the risks of not trying are inertia—paralysis. If there's a path away from the chasm of self-doubt, take it! Staying in a rut is "comfortable" but passive.'

"Leave the path of least resistance—*act*! Add to yourself, don't subtract! Simplify your choices. Lighten the load by removing the garbage, by not worrying about the future, by not wasting energy in conformity.

"If others don't seem to understand or value you, understand and value yourself. Are you standing in the way of yourself? If so, stand aside.

"I repeated some words I had once written: 'Take up the kaleidoscope that is your life, shake it a little, then look again. Wow! A whole new perspective, an awesome view.'

"If lost in the woods, I suggested, do *not* retrace your own footsteps. Look up, follow your star. Accept that the way, though far and hard, will lead you home.

"From the standpoint of my own failed marriage, would that I had once had these words. They might have shown me the true meaning of 'ego.' Hindsight? Maybe, but more comforting . . . *insight*.

"Did Alison hear me? Well, she married happily, at age thirty-three, in her own good time."

Miami thrust an oppressive awareness on me—as if Marley's Ghost and the Spirit of Christmas Yet to Come had turned my face to what I was becoming under that tropical sky. Someone else. Someone I didn't like.

Soon after moving back to Portland, I purchased a copy of the American Psychiatric Association's *Diagnostic and Statistical Manual of Mental Disorders*. This manual is the psychotherapist's bible of dysfunctional behavior, a wonderful resource for novelists attempting to flesh out their fictional characters. Thumbing through the manual one day, I came across a description of Histrionic Personality Disorder (HPD):

"Individuals with HPD are uncomfortable or feel unappreciated when they are not the center of attention. Often lively and dramatic, they tend to draw attention to themselves and may initially charm new acquaintances by their enthusiasm, apparent openness or flirtatiousness. These qualities wear thin, however, as these individuals continually demand to be the center of attention. They commandeer the role of 'the life of the party.' If they are not the center of attention, they may do something dramatic to draw the focus of attention to themselves."

And I recognized myself.

A few pages later, I encountered the diagnostic features of a Narcissistic Personality Disorder (NPD):

"Individuals with NPD have a grandiose sense of self-importance. They routinely overestimate their abilities and inflate their accomplishments, often appearing boastful and pretentious. They may blithely assume that others attribute the same value to their efforts and may be surprised when the praise they expect and feel they deserve is not forthcoming. Often implicit in the inflated judgments of their own accomplishments is an underestimation (devaluation) of the contributions of others. They are often preoccupied with fantasies of unlimited success, power, brilliance, beauty, or ideal love. They may ruminate about 'long overdue' admiration and privilege and compare themselves favorably with famous or privileged people."

And I recognized myself again. So I quit reading.

Then I realized that these diagnoses fit virtually every successful person in the world, particularly those household names in big business, politics, and show biz, along with most of the marketing, advertising, and public relations personalities I'd ever worked with.

And why not, when every book in the how-to-succeed genre encourages this sort of over-the-top, in-your-face conceit as a prerequisite on the high road to fame and fortune? Sheer, runaway egotism, I realized in dismay, is the linchpin of the engine that drives personal and professional achievement.

Shaken to the core by this revelation of myself in a manual of mental disorders, I immediately began my twelve-step Ego Abatement Program. Six years later, I have reached the fourth rung down from the precipitous descent from the heights of my conceit. Progress is slow, tedious, discouraging. I stumble and fall, but I press on, fighting my battles one day at a time, inching ever closer to that blessed state of egolessness.

———————

There's good news and bad news in distancing yourself from people. The bad news is that your phone doesn't ring much anymore. The good news is that when it does ring, someone who matters is calling, someone who cares enough about you to make the effort.

Moving to a faraway place, so friends have to take pen or mouse or phone in hand to stay close, lets you know which of the people you hung onto for so long consider you disposable, of far lesser importance to them than you believed. The worthwhile ones stick despite the distance and expense. The rest fall away. Call it a friendship litmus test.

Want to do something good for yourself and a friend or two who've drifted away? Pick up the phone one day and call. Don't wait till you need something. Just call and say, "I was thinking about you. How's it going?"

You'll hang up feeling good. So will your friend.

In a quid pro quo world, nonreciprocal gifts are rare.

This is something solitaires know.

Look up "encumbrance" in your thesaurus. You'll find heavy words: weight, impediment, burden, hindrance. Now look up "disencumber." The synonyms are airy, liberating: lighten, relax, relieve, abate.

"The deliberate simplification of our lives should not be equated with turning away from progress," sums up *Voluntary Simplicity* author Duane Elgin. "To the contrary, simplicity is crucial to progress, for without simplicity we will be overwhelmed by massive social and material complexity."

"To simplify is to bring order, clarity, and purpose into our lives."

A typical day in the southern metropolis in which Laura Lang lives and works is "filled with heavy traffic, noisy people at work playing political games to get ahead, and a constant barrage of information for me to take action on," says the single, forty-two-year-old marketing executive.

"When I get home, the first thing I do is go outside. I sit and I listen. I smell and I feel. I think there's so much comfort in nature that people don't take advantage of.

"I listen to the wind in the trees. I listen to the birds talking to each other. I smell the grass. I smell the rain coming. I feel the wind around me. I use as many senses as I can. I relax. I get centered so I can face the next day."

I thought of Lang and smiled when I saw a cartoon in the morning paper. It showed an executive at his desk, in an office with windows surrounded by skyscrapers. The man is holding a potted plant as he instructs his secretary over the intercom, "No calls for a while, Helen. I'm communing with nature."

> *"When I get home, the first thing I do is go outside. I sit and I listen. I smell and I feel. I think there's so much comfort in nature that people don't take advantage of."*

It is the silence Jeri Beasley cherishes most. Even now, after eighteen years of living alone following a seven-year marriage that ended when she was thirty, the forty-eight-year-old lawyer goes on silent retreats at a nearby abbey. "It's a unique experience taking in silence with others," she says.

"I can meditate, be quiet inside, listen to God, and yet be with people. After several days, I feel I know them intimately, even though we've never spoken."

Her marriage was not a happy one, Beasley reveals. "It was a relief to finally end it. I loved being single again. I loved the freedom to come and go without anyone to account to. I loved being in my own space, doing whatever I wanted to do in complete stillness—staring at the wall, gazing out at the river, puttering aimlessly, folding laundry—hands working, mind thinking."

She spends an hour "in prayer and meditation" every morning and evening, combined with "times of quiet" during the day. "The silence lets me examine my expectations, my dreams, but the silence is healing whether I'm thinking or not."

Still, she's not ready for complete solitude, she says.

"I need to socialize, feel connected, but only for so long, then I have to pull back. By the same token, I live in a different part of myself, a deeper part, and I sometimes need to take a break from that."

Beasley gave up practicing law when her parents died and left her with a "comfortable" inheritance. Since then, she's used the economic freedom to do volunteer work, turning it into a new full-time career.

"It's important for me to be doing worthwhile things," she says.

She's grateful to the money for that reason—not for what it's enabled her to purchase. "I have no desire to own my home," she says. "I feel it would just tie me down."

Instead, she's lived for the past nine years in a three-bedroom apartment across the hall from the larger one she moved into after her divorce. "I didn't need the space," she explains.

She also drives an '84 Honda with almost 112,000 miles on the odometer. "I'm very conscious about not replacing things until I've used them up."

Yet, she enjoys shopping immensely, she reveals, just not *buying*. "I love to look at things in shop windows without any desire whatsoever to own them. It would make me feel 'heavy' having to be responsible for something else. I'm content with what I have."

In conclusion, Beasley offers a quote from Alexander Stoddard: "Life is too short to be taking care of the wrong details."

Whenever she repeats the words, she says, she adds one of her own: "Amen."

Chapter Twelve

In Search of Validity:
Truth, Authenticity, Self

Believing in life before *death is*
hard enough.
—"Shoe," the comic strip crow

We sit on the side porch of Sarah Winthrop's Montana home. Around us the Rocky Mountains form a spectacular backdrop under the huge Western sky. She points at the horses that have returned to the corral from the pasture and stand waiting, watching us. The day is cooling swiftly.

Winthrop gets up abruptly, gives a rope tied to one of the porch columns a sharp tug that sets a cow bell clanging. The bell is hung on the limb of a tree between the house and the stables. She rings it, she says, to scare off a fox that's constantly on the prowl for her bantam chickens when they're loose in the yard.

She has to start her evening chores, she informs me, pulling on a pair of cowhide work gloves, but she would be happy to talk while she works. I walk with her in the fading light, and she resumes telling me about a life she chose—which became the life that chose her.

"It was more my quest than his," says Winthrop, fifty-one, a Montanan since 1979, the summer she and her ex-husband quit their jobs in Long Island, New York, and headed west. "We came out cold—no jobs, no prospects, enough money to live six months." They had originally set their sights on a small college town in the Rockies but wound up instead in a ramshackle rented house in a canyon thirty miles from town.

"We could have died that first Montana winter, and no one would have found us until spring," she says with a laugh, then adds, "They say God loves fools and children. He must have included two greenhorns from New York that year."

But things worked out. Her husband found work almost immediately in the business office of a local health club. She landed a job three months later at the local university, where she still works. They divorced two years later. He moved to Florida. She stayed on in Montana with their two-year-old daughter, bought a house set on twenty acres, had a 1,400-square-foot barn built, and began filling the place with animals.

There are enough of them now to stock a children's zoo. She never intended to wind up with so many, she says, but couldn't turn any of them away. "I tend to take in older, unwanted animals. I care for them and let them exit gracefully, knowing they're loved."

Winthrop tells me about each one of them as she rakes and shovels manure in the stable, hauling each wheelbarrow load into an adjoining pasture, then spreads fresh hay in the stalls and puts fresh grain in the buckets before bringing in the horses, talking gently to each as she leads them inside for the night.

"My animals stay with me until they die. They're inconvenient, cost money, and require much of me, but they're not disposable—not one of them," she says sternly.

She owns four horses: Patriot, a thirty-year-old thoroughbred gelding; Aspen, twenty-one, her ex-husband's sorrel mare; Mocha, thirteen, Aspen's Appaloosa daughter, born thirteen years ago in Winthrop's barn; and Samilla, a seven-year-old Spanish Arabian gelding. There are two more horses buried in the southwest corner of her pasture, she says, plus several dogs and numerous other pets that lived out their lives under her care.

She tells about her cats, fourteen of them, providing their ages along with their names. There's Macho and Ebby, both seventeen; Mary, fifteen; Merlin and Shadow, both fourteen; Adam, Chelsea, and Lily, all thirteen; Annie, twelve; Pooter, Amber, and Jake, all seven; and Squeak and Tom, both two.

The dogs are named Scruffy, fifteen; Zucchini and Thumper, both ten; and Muffy. ("I have no idea of her age—she looks old but has young teeth.") They were adopted from the local animal shelter, she says. The cats were either strays or abandoned on the dirt road leading to her property because people knew she would take them in.

"I keep the names they're used to. They come with their own identities, characteristics, and behaviors. I try to live with them as individuals."

Winthrop continues with her inventory of pets: two cockatiels, Beauregard, twelve, and Luna, six; a three-year-old dwarf Dutch rabbit named Lucy; four hamsters salvaged from a school classroom; Emma, a five-year-old 105-pound Vietnamese pot-bellied pig with "a very strong personality" and her own heated pig condo; six bantam chickens (two roosters, four hens) answering to Winston, Roosevelt, Rosie, Dolly, Topaz, and Silver; and two geese she calls Willie and Wally.

Her current list of adopted animals totals more than thirty—she's had as many as forty at a time—and I marvel at her familiarity with and loving characterization of each one. She's up at 5:30 each morning to feed and care for them before fixing her daughter's school lunch and dressing for her 8-to-4 job at the university.

"I probably spend the least time on myself," says Winthrop. "I tend to wear the same clothes over and over, usually rush to work with alfalfa in my hair."

At work, she occasionally gets a phone call informing her that one or another of her pets is up to something requiring immediate intervention. "I once spent two hours on the roof of my house with a pair of binoculars," she says, "looking for Emma after a neighbor alerted me the pig had wandered off."

She hasn't figured out how much she spends each year on her animals, but the sum must be sizable. In addition to the endless bales of hay that she grows herself, the grain for the horses, the pig feed, dog and cat chow, and esoteric other critter vittles add up to a tidy sum at year's end.

Inevitably, there are also the bills for medical care, surgery, and medicine. Patriot, the thirty-year-old gelding, has a dozen staples above his left eye, the result of an encounter with a stationary object in the pasture, she informs, as I watch her inject a shot of penicillin into the horse's rump, then spray his wound with an antibiotic.

"I've never sat down and figured out what the animals cost me each year," Winthrop says, smiling wryly at the thought of even trying. "I'd rather not know." She shrugs. "To lead this life, you need to do what has to be done. My love for them is enough reason."

I ask her what the animals give her in return. "Authenticity is a word that comes to mind," she replies.

Winthrop yanks the rope attached to the cow bell as she passes it on our way back to the house, then continues.

"I think my life genuinely belongs to me. I seriously doubt the niche I've carved for myself could have been arrived at as a joint decision, but it's a genuine life, whether I chose it or it chose me. Was I fated for my destiny? Perhaps, but I like to view it more as paying attention and giving a voice and action to that which I feel strongly about—nurturing and caring for the furred and feathered creatures we share our planet with. They have an existence too, and we have to honor that."

"My life would be a hell of a lot simpler without these animals," Winthrop adds. "There would be a lot less emotional pain for me. They're certainly demanding, no doubt about it, but that's because they're dependent on a human for their basic needs, unlike the wildlife that's so abundant in this state. They require time, energy, and commitment, but I've learned so much about living and dying by being with them."

"There's definitely a lot of spontaneity in the animal world, and I like to think they keep me open, expectant, and accepting as well. Besides, they're tremendously good company—always fun to be around and to observe, not to mention a great source of anecdotal material to share with my human companions."

> "I think my life genuinely belongs to me. I seriously doubt the niche I've carved for myself could have been arrived at as a joint decision, but it's a genuine life, whether I chose it or it chose me."

Winthrop loves the rural setting she's chosen, she says. "The quiet is food for my soul. Being in the country, taking care of the animals—sometimes I joke that this is a full-time moonlighting job for which I don't receive any monetary benefits—has brought me an acceptance of the natural world as it exists. And that's worth infinitely more to me than money."

In making her choices, Winthrop concludes, she's tried her utmost to honor her most deeply held feelings and beliefs. "I'm on a solo journey called life. I can't imagine why I'd want to take my cues from anyone but me. I live with my choices so I can rejoice and not hold anyone but me accountable for the outcome."

Cheri Isleworth, fifty-five, describes herself as a "quasi-hermit-writer-idealist," who for the past fifteen years has opted out of a culture that says, in her words, "More is better! Gimme! Gimme more stuff!"

"As a result," says Isleworth, "I've lived beyond frugal—quite honestly, below the poverty line. But in so doing, I've awakened to the truths about what living an examined life means in the context of simplifying, simplifying, simplifying."

After a couple of disastrous marriages, Isleworth reveals, the time came for her to look inside herself. "And look inside myself I did. This kind of reflection—for me a least—had to be done alone. And it continues to be a solitary undertaking."

She is never lonely, she claims. "Alone, I began to listen to those subtle and provocative curiosities that had been a part of me since childhood. Introverted, intellectually and spiritually curious, I finally began the most important work of my life as a human being."

"I embarked on a thorough, honest, deliberate evaluation of who I was and where and how I fit in the world. What I found in those abandoned, forgotten parts of myself continues to amaze and startle me at times. Intuitive by nature, I began to *listen* to those messages that seemed to arrive abruptly and without warning.

"And I began at last to feel as if I'd returned to my center. That I'd finally come home."

Before his divorce, before the many years of therapy that followed, before all the drastic changes that he knew he would have to make, Roy Morris thought he had life squarely by the horns.

Married for nineteen years, with an attractive wife, two sons, and two daughters, the forty-seven-year-old corporate communications director earned a handsome salary, drove a late-model car, and owned a large home in the suburbs.

"I thought I was doing everything just right," he says. "And I got sicker and sicker."

Single for the past four years, now living with his thirteen-year-old son in a small house closer to the city, Morris works from his home as a freelance writer. "I was scared and panicky," he says, recounting his spiraling free fall before yanking the rip cord six years ago.

"I started getting goofy thoughts, and then panic disorders followed by a number of physical problems—esophageal spasms, physical exhaustion, an inner-ear disorder that caused dizziness under stress—all of which I blithely hid from everyone, including myself, behind a facade of carefree normalcy."

Driving to work in the morning, says Morris, he found it harder and harder to get on the freeway. "I had this irrational fear that I wouldn't be able to get off again, that I'd be stuck there forever. I found it hard to like myself, to feel good about anything I was doing. It seemed there was nothing and no one I could relate to anymore."

When his dizzy spells became more frequent, he went to a series of doctors, one of whom finally sent him on to a psychotherapist. Soon afterwards, he quit his job. "I just left one day," he says.

"I didn't work for six months, told everyone I was 'sick.' I stayed home, grew a beard, listened to music. One day, I bought a pack of cigarettes after quitting for four years and started smoking again. I thought a lot about myself as a child, how I spent so much time in the basement of our house, reading, playing the piano, sketching. I remembered that I always needed time for myself as a kid."

One day, he got on a plane and flew to New Jersey to visit a Navy buddy he'd served with in Vietnam. "I had a great time," he says. "I felt I'd turned the clock back eighteen years, that I'd found an old friend—the person who used to be *me*—that I'd lost complete touch with myself and somehow had made glorious contact again. I was amazed—exhilarated!—and I decided I had to preserve that feeling at all costs."

"My wife couldn't stand the new me, of course. She was angry and perplexed, particularly when counseling didn't help. The person she'd married—the diligent, conscientious, hard-working family man, and corporate executive whom she'd worked so hard to mold—was suddenly gone. Nine months later, we were divorced."

He thought seriously of moving into a cabin in the mountains, but realized he couldn't sever all contact with his children. "Instead," says Morris, "I started doing something I hadn't done since I was a kid, and that was to enjoy myself, to live my life so it made sense to me, to do the work I was comfortable doing and that gave me pleasure. I began looking forward to being by myself, not talking to anyone but clients for long periods of time. I started writing music—church hymns, something I'd wanted to do for a long time."

His deliberate solitude wasn't "peaceful," Morris says, but "wild and crazy." He would jump from one thing to the next, completing projects with intense, exuberant bursts of energy, totally exhausting himself, and then spend days doing nothing, "just daydreaming—getting wild ideas."

He has found out a few things about himself, he says. Primary among them is the simple fact that he doesn't enjoy being with people as much as he enjoys being by himself.

> "I started doing something I hadn't done since I was a kid, and that was to enjoy myself, to live my life so it made sense to me, to do the work I was comfortable doing and that gave me pleasure."

He knows now that when he was out there supposedly having "fun" with others, he really wasn't, that he actually dreaded and "got through" most of his obligatory social obligations. As a successful high-tech freelance writer, much in demand, he shuns all but the most necessary of meetings, conducting all his business by phone, fax, modem, and E-mail.

If he's sad or lonely or feeling emotional stress, he'll write a note—and send it or not. "Either way, I feel I've been with someone," he says. "Yet there's a part of me that's completely aloof, not in a snooty sense, but I've learned I don't need to share all my problems with people, that I can't bare my soul or even want to."

And so he's whittled his social activities down to two groups, he says. The first is his church, which he chose "far from home, clear across town." The second is his Vietnam Veterans of America group, which holds meetings once a month. Why these? "Because they're safe," he replies.

I wait for him to say more, to explain what he means, but he doesn't.

He seldom dates anymore, he reveals. "I'm not consistent with most things. I can only take people in small doses. I'm good for a day or a week, then I have to move on. I make sure I don't get into something I can't get out of quickly."

Why bother at all? "Venturing out into 'safe' things is a way of confirming myself," he replies. "I don't do it because I'm lonely. I do it for reinforcement. So that when I come back to myself, I know exactly who that person is."

Four years after my interview with the hermit of Dead Cow Gulch in Santa Fe, I phoned Susan Baumgartner to ask her which fork in the road she had wound up taking in her journey to herself. On the second ring, a man answered, identifying himself as Sean Gardner. I didn't recognize the name but the deep, friendly voice was familiar. When I told him who I was and asked to talk to Susan, Gardner laughed.

"Speaking," he said.

"A week after you visited with Susan in the fall of 1996," Gardner then explained to me good-naturedly, "Sean replaced her, after repressing his real identity for twenty-two years."

He was first diagnosed as a female-to-male transsexual in 1978, Gardner then told me. He had planned on making the full transition to his male self back then and actually began the massive infusions of testosterone. "But I couldn't do it," he said. "I was twenty-six years old, there was no support group, no such thing as a gender community where I lived. I didn't even know any lesbians or gay men."

Instead, he lived as a hermit in the North Idaho wilderness to avoid the confusion and compulsively wrote novels with male protagonists. "And I tried to be a lesbian—I really tried. I worked to liberate myself from my internalized misogyny. I tried to overcome my patriarchal upbringing. I worshiped my lesbian friends, their womanly beauty, their strength, and courage in being themselves. I threw myself into the life of the lesbian and gay community, and I fought in the trenches against the ignorance and bigotry."

"But it wasn't enough," Gardner said.

As a lesbian, she'd had a relationship with another woman. Life had been better, but it was never right for the woman who had spent her entire life feeling like a man. The headlong escapes into solitude and writing—the endless hours of self-examination—the desperate attempts at acceptance and reconciliation in search of peace had all failed.

It was then that she received an invitation from her sister to move to Santa Fe for a year and take on the part-time job of caring for her sister's two young daughters. A new, vastly different place might help, her sister reasoned. The salary would support her and she'd be able to write whenever she wasn't caring for the girls. Baumgartner consented.

On the June 1996 weekend before she departed for Santa Fe, Baumgartner attended a "We Are Family" youth conference at Washington State University. One of the highlights of the conference was David Harrison's performance of his play, *FTM*, which Baumgartner took in.

"And my life blew up in my face," Gardner said.

"There he was up on the stage, dramatizing his transition from Catherine to David," Gardner went on, "every aspect of his story exactly fitting every aspect of mine. Flattened into my seat by the power of his performance, the realization struck me like a thunderbolt, that biology didn't have to be destiny. Like Harrison, I could complete the terrifying, exhilarating journey to my true self."

And so Susan Baumgartner departed her magical cabin at Dead Cow Gulch, shaken to the core of her being, although she gave no indication of the depth of her feelings or her resurrected resolve to become a man when I talked with her in Santa Fe several weeks later.

Honoring her commitment to her sister, she took care of her two nieces through the following June before launching a search for a "real" job in technical writing and editing. But the pile of resumes Baumgartner sent out proved fruitless, and she started doing temp work for several agencies in town, filling in occasionally as a nanny for the two girls.

That same June, a year after leaving Idaho, she returned to be the maid of honor at her sister Annie's wedding, wearing "a lavender dress, shoes dyed to match, the works. It was my swan song as Susan."

The massive self-administered infusions of testosterone began, followed by the extremely painful operations in Montreal, the first in January of 1998 to remove the fat, lymph nodes, and ducts from her chest, then a double mastectomy several months later, followed by reconstructive surgery to create a male chest.

And so Sean Gardner was born. He hopes to have a hysterectomy, which his insurance doesn't cover. Also, he's not sure when he'll be able to afford the costly, still-unrefined surgery to create the rest of his new body. But the pain has all been physical, Gardner makes it clear. "A lot of people told me there would be a grieving period," he said of his change. "For me, it was pure joy. And a huge relief. The only sadness is for all the years I missed. It's almost like all that came before has been obliterated. I feel so lucky now."

He also has a renewed appreciation for the sense of humor that's always sustained him, Gardner said, because there's such a great need for it occasionally. "For instance, I was picking up a prescription recently, and the male pharmacist called the female pharmacist over for a consultation. They're chatting away and he's addressing me as 'she' while she's addressing me as 'he' and though it's weirding me out, they seem oblivious to their conflicting interpretations of who or what I am."

Gardner shrugs, laughs, adds softly, "All that matters is that I know who and what I am, that I've become the person I was always meant to be."

And he's grateful that the deep, comforting connection to solitude he had for so long is back, stronger than ever. "It disappeared for nearly three years, during that period of my life when I was preoccupied with such things as changing my gender," Gardner said.

"Then just when I thought I'd changed so incontrovertibly that solitude was no longer necessary or even possible for me, it returned, subtly but insistently, like a silent, wonderful gift. What a gratifying surprise to learn that solitude was an integral part of the me I carried from Susan to Sean, the core being that gives my life an essential thread of continuity despite the radical changes," Gardner added.

"I think my desire for solitude came most strongly from the male part of myself, from the need to go down into the cave, from the masculine toughness that makes me want to fight things out on my own."

His increasing departures from solitude into the social aspects of his new life are more comfortable to him now because of his ease with himself, Gardner said. "But when work or weekend activities end, I'm the one with the smile on my face heading home."

Home used to be the $9' \times 12'$ foot cabin in the middle of nowhere. Now it's the middle apartment in a line of three, a twenty-minute walk from downtown Santa Fe. "It's barely larger than the cabin and quite old and funky," said Gardner, "but it does have some amazing creature comforts such as electricity, indoor plumbing, central heating, E-mail, and a phone."

"Still, in spite of all the civilization and people around me, I find it amazingly easy to reach a transcendent state of aloneness, as if the years of solitude at the cabin were so intense they laid a well-worn path of synapses and relays in my brain, providing a familiar shortcut."

"Triggers from nature still help and, fortunately, Santa Fe, though growing rapidly, retains a village feel to it, at least in some areas. The sight of a branch on an apricot tree arching into the blue sky will do it. Or golden fruit growing succulent in the sun, the intoxicating scent of wet earth on those rare days when rain comes to this desert land. It can be something as simple as the touch of mountain air wafting through a window," Gardner continued.

"Solitude has become the food that makes me my best self. In my solitude, the smallest act is imbued with intense pleasure. Everything, including the most menial of household tasks, becomes art. Time stretches itself and I move within it at the pace most comfortable for me.

"I think about real things, not what I'll have for dinner or when I need to pay my bills, but how the essay I just read resonates with the way things are in my world or how watching my niece yesterday helped me clarify some buried misunderstanding from my childhood.

"I can't believe my incredible good fortune, that I get to live in a wonderful mental space that expands and transforms whatever physical confines I happen to find myself in. I can't imagine how people without access to this miraculous place of respite and deepened awareness can survive. Yet, they seem to sense its wonder.

"One of the ironies of being a successful solitary is that people are drawn to me. They perceive a solidity, a central, peaceful core that most of them don't have. And I find myself fending them off, because if I give in to the constant barrage of interaction and motion and noise that most people endure, I would lose the quality they find so compelling.

> "Solitude has become the food that makes me my best self. In my solitude, the smallest act is imbued with intense pleasure. Everything, including the most menial of household tasks, becomes art.

"I want to tell them they can't have their solidity by siphoning it from me. It doesn't come from the outside. They have to find it in themselves.

"Despite all I've discovered about myself, though, there's something that is still a mystery to me, a burning question, the answer to which I yet don't know: Can I have all the space and solitude I seem to need and also the fulfillment of a relationship?

"It isn't that, with my new gender and this new body, I still feel a bit insecure about love and romance and sex. The question is much more elemental: Because of the very nature of solitude and the relationships that infringe on it, is it possible to have both? Can a life incorporating solitude and togetherness be as rich and rewarding as the more conventional life, whether gay or straight?

"Whatever the answer, I still revel in my solitude. I love having it back. I love being able to count on it once more. I love the strength it generates because it pushes me to deal fully with the essentials of life, those things which, though harsh and elemental, are grounding and ultimately most transcendent. I feel like the luckiest man in the world to have a congruent gender, the fulfillment of writing, the joy of having myself when that is all there is.

"What more could anyone possibly want?"

Well, perhaps one thing. "The success of my first novel, *Missionary,* would be nice," he said. "It's a sci-fi epic set in the year 2052, and takes a new look at that hoary old battle between science and religion. Part of the conflict of the story revolves around the struggles of the main character, Mica, to balance his love of solitude with his desire to connect with those around him."

I think I saw that one coming, I told him.

Chapter Thirteen

The Way of the Curmudgeon:
Better Living Through Eccentricity

Curmudgeons are like sumo
wrestlers; it takes a long time and a
lot of abuse to make one.
—JON WINOKUR

I like curmudgeons. I admire them. In fact, I think of myself as one, even though you're really not one until someone else says you are, claims Jon Winokur, editor and compiler of *The Portable Curmudgeon*.

I realized I was a curmudgeon when I read Winokur's collection of "irreverent observations by world-class grouches" and found myself applauding everything they said. Winokur knew he was one when he developed a permanent sneer, found he'd lost his taste for "anything cute and trendy," and realized he was increasingly out of step with everyone and everything around him.

I think my youngest son, Andy, has also become a curmudgeon at the tender age of twenty-nine, the result of massive force-feedings of the story of man in his pursuit of a Ph.D. in American history. Reading too much too soon about our track record on earth can make a curmudgeon out of anyone.

As can living alone. For solitude lets us see ourselves plainly—a prerequisite to befriending, understanding, and eventually loving that person we finally allow ourselves to be.

And because we see ourselves plainly at last, we are able see others plainly as well. Because we no longer accept dishonesty in ourselves, we no longer tolerate it in others. Because we can't lie to ourselves, we don't allow others to lie to us. Which is why curmudgeons don't suffer fools wisely.

Or humbugs, hypocrites, charlatans, impostors, or liars, for that matter—particularly liars.

Curmudgeons are cockeyed optimists who have finally started to see straight. They're the fools who rushed in where angels feared to tread before realizing what quicksand could do. They're the eternal romantics told to get *real*. Turned into doubting Thomases, they now have to let the world know how things really are.

Curmudgeons tell the truth as they see it because they *have* to. It's both their punishment and reward for finally summoning the courage to face themselves.

What they fail to understand, however, is that most people can't *handle* the truth, not when it comes from others; that few will accept, much less appreciate, the absurdity of the human condition when it's rubbed in their faces; and that truth is something we need to tell ourselves, to find in our own hearts, to hear directly from God during long walks on the beach.

Traditionally, too, the American Dream of fame, fortune, business success, and political ascendancy has come from telling others what they want to hear, not what they *need* to hear. Those of us, therefore, who want to get along shouldn't insist on telling people what they don't want to hear, which is what curmudgeons are compelled to do, and which is why their compulsive honesty is at once a blessing and a curse.

Nonetheless, after a lifetime of biting their tongues because their jobs, raises, promotions, domestic tranquility, and public personae have relied on their forced equanimity, "putting a sock in it" no longer works for curmudgeons. Telling the truth regardless of the consequences has become crucially important to them, and as natural as it was when they were children.

Contrary to popular opinion, curmudgeons come in all ages and both sexes, for their condition is a state of mind rather than age or gender. They're as softhearted and sensitive as the next person, claims Winokur, but they hide their vulnerability under a crust of misanthropy. Seeing themselves and the world clearly at last, they feel your pain and try to ease it by turning hurt into humor.

"They snarl at pretense and bite at hypocrisy out of a healthy sense of outrage," says Winokur. "They attack maudlinism because it devalues genuine sentiment. They hurl polemical thunderbolts at middle-class values and pop culture in order to preserve their sanity."

So be kind to a curmudgeon today.

When it finally dawns on you that you're married to one, or your boss or best friend is one, or you find yourself trapped in a window seat next to one on a transatlantic flight, be nice. Appreciate them for who they are and how they got that way. And one day, when someone calls *you* a curmudgeon, smile and reply, "Why, how nice of you to say so."

The only real curmudgeon I know has become my best friend at the beach. His full name, he told me on the day that we met six years ago, is Alberto Joaquin Villareal Terego. "Teh-*reh*-go," he pronounced his last name for me, emphasis on the second syllable. "But you can call me Alberto." I liked him immediately.

A man about my age, though he looks much younger, he was married for many years as I was, has several children and grandchildren in distant cities as I do, and now lives alone on the peninsula. Invariably cheerful, possessed of a self-deprecating sense of humor, and usually seen strolling with his dog by the surf where the day is coolest, Terego is always a welcome sight to me and Buddy.

A thoughtful man living an examined life in the fullest sense, Terego seems to enjoy my company as well. Over the years, we've discussed virtually everything under the sun during our countless walks by the sea. Because he's an insatiable reader with a storehouse of timeless quotes, he's an entertaining and astute conversationalist who usually drives home his points in other people's words.

The other day, for instance, I made the remark, "You gotta do what you gotta do." He replied with an old German proverb that stated the same fact much more eloquently: "One must carve one's life out of the wood one has."

Or if I say something like, "Most people are ambivalent about solitude," he'll counter with a pungent line, such as Susan Ertz's classic observation: "Millions long for immortality who don't know what to do with themselves on a rainy Sunday afternoon."

If he weren't so articulate, he'd be a pain-in-the-butt know-it-all. Needless to say, I enjoy him immensely.

Naturally, a favorite subject for both of us is our solitary lifestyle. We've talked at length about the guilt Americans seem to feel over wanting to be alone. "It's not surprising, in that our greatest social conflict stems from our most deeply held value: the freedom to be left alone," Terego says.

"Trouble is, while we're a nation that resists having other people's ideas and lifestyles forced on us, we're also a society that nurtures intimacy, interdependence, and a responsibility for our fellow man. The difficulty lies in reconciling those polar desires: our yearning for independence with our commitment to others."

Paramount to individual fulfillment is a strong sense of self-reliance, he notes, but assuming full responsibility for one's emotional well-being implies a stronger attachment to self than to family, interpersonal relationships, and the traditional demands of society. Aloneness is a threatening concept to most Americans because we've been brought up to believe that our fulfillment lies in others; that, whatever the cost, they are essential to the equation; that, without them, our lives simply don't add up.

Even our heroes have always had sidekicks: Don Quixote and Sancho Panza, Crusoe and Friday, Batman and Robin, the Green Hornet and Kato, Thelma and Louise. And so we marvel at the Lone Rangers without their Tontos.

"The conflict emerges," Terego says, "when making ourselves the best that we can be makes us not as good for others. This is discomforting to those whose happiness has always been predicated on making *others* happy—first and foremost. Feeling good versus *being* good is a New Age conundrum to many embarking on their long-delayed quests for self-actualization—journeys taking them away from others in search of themselves."

Just as disturbing to sociologists, psychologists, and society as a whole is the thought that a population of self-seekers may be forming a "culture of separation," adds Terego.

In *Habits of the Heart*, the best-selling study of American society by Robert N. Bellah, Richard Madsen, William M. Sullivan, Ann Swidler, and Steven M. Tipton, the authors suggest that "finding oneself" (also known as "romantic individualism") is merely a fad fostered by pop culture and the media, particularly television. If this culture of separation ever became dominant, they assure us, it would "collapse of its own incoherence."

These five sociologists also dismiss the humanistic assumption that at the core of every individual is a fundamental spiritual harmony that links each of us—not only to every other person, but to the cosmos and everything in it. And that with the discovery and affirmation of self comes a oneness with the universe.

"Such romantic individualism," they scoff, "is remarkably thin when it comes to any but the vaguest prescriptions about how to live in an actual society."

Perhaps. But I still prefer Thomas Moore's views on the need for both attachment and detachment in the spiritual quest for ourselves. "If we have strong desires to have a family, live with another person, or join a community, but find, after these desires have been satisfied, that we are drawn in exactly the opposite direction, then we might remember that this complexity is simply the way of the soul," enjoins the prolific author of *Soul Mates*.

> "We may have to look for concrete ways to give life to both sides of the spectrum, enjoying both our intimacies and our solitude."

"We may have to look for concrete ways to give life to both sides of the spectrum, enjoying both our intimacies and our solitude."

In the novel *Toots in Solitude*, John Yount's wry, sweet fable about identity, commitment, and the essence of love, Macon "Toots" Henslee has left his wife and the cares of the world to live in serenity and joy in a treehouse near a river—his own person in every way. But into his life comes Sally Ann, a would-be country singer fleeing her drug-dealer lover with $250,000 of his cash in tow. Their relationship, before its inevitable end, is poignant and immensely appealing. The novel closes with these poetic lines:

"But a little at a time, sweet solitude began to visit him again. Oh, but she was jealous, was solitude, and wouldn't come near if any thought of Sally Ann was in his head, and would withdraw if one of her aspects caused him to think, however fleetingly, of her rival. But by the time the first chilling winter had passed and there were silver sprays of catkins in the marsh willows, she kept his company. After all, she demanded only that he be faithful and not one thing more."

As a solitary curmudgeon, there are things I no longer do at the beach. Shave every day. Wash my car. Balance my checkbook. Worry. Buy into or try to figure out other people's foolishness and hidden agendas. Sweat the small, medium, or even large stuff—just the monumental impending events on my very short list.

I have no trouble with people trying to be Martha Stewart-perfect, only with those who do it for everyone but themselves.

And I've whittled down the Ten Commandments of my guilt-ridden Roman Catholic youth to three: I. To thine own self be true. II. Try never to hurt anyone again. III. When necessary, break Commandment II to achieve Commandment I.

Personally, I think Moses blew it when he descended Sinai with all those "Shalt Nots" engraved on the two tablets of stone. Halfway down the mountain, he should have tossed them, then told the waiting throng below, "Listen up, people, God has just one commandment for you: Be kind." It would have been enough.

A few other lessons solitude has taught me:

If it's not worth overdoing, don't bother. As an obsessive-compulsive personality, my motto has always been, "If it's worth doing, it's worth overdoing." But alone at the beach, I've amended that cardinal rule to read, "If it's not worth overdoing, don't bother." This assures me enough time to overdo everything on my extremely short list. And to be passionate about whatever I happen to be doing.

Too many of our problems stem from people who merely go through the motions, doing only what they need to do to get by. There ought to be a law that says that if you don't care enough to give it your very best, then you don't get to try at all. And if it takes getting rid of all the people and all the things you don't really care about in order to be passionate about the people and things that are left, well, that's OK too.

How sad, though, that we wait most of our lives to come up with a short list.

Codependent tennis is not a good game. When you serve the ball, someone should hit it back to you. If no one tries, the match should be over as far as you're concerned. Put your racket away, go home, find another game tomorrow. Stop returning your own serves, lobs, and volleys. Stop playing off your own energy, needs, and desires. Quit kidding yourself.

The 10-percenters will always be with us. Half a lifetime ago at the U.S. Marine Corps Depot in Parris Island, South Carolina, where they took my soft, undisciplined body and forged it into a finely tuned war machine, a drill instructor named Karl Minnick enlightened me on the 10-percenters of the world.

"No matter how often and efficiently I put out the word," he snarled at me one blistering sand-flea-infested afternoon, eyes livid, breath scalding, flaring nostrils centimeters from my quavering features, "10 percent of you motherless cretins won't get with the program. Just pray, boy, you're never one of them!"

I've cleaned up his language a bit, but that was the gist of my DI's benign counsel, except that I've made it a 40-percent, occasionally a 60- or 90-percent rule. What Sgt. Minnick meant was that regardless of how much you threaten, beg, bully, or cajole any group of people into doing something, no matter what the rewards or consequences, there will *always* be those who won't get with the program. Don't take it personally; it's just one of life's imponderables that you'll have to accept.

So save yourself a lot of grief and factor the 10-percenters into everything you do, for they will always be with us.

Don't pray for God's sake, pray for your own. He doesn't need your prayers, but you do. Well, maybe not you. I pray a lot at the beach—much more than I ever did in the city. But I do it for my sake now, not God's. Funny that it took me so long to realize that simple need, to get it turned right-side-out in my head.

Do it for yourself. If it winds up being good for others, that's fine too. If not, it won't matter because you'll have done it for yourself in the first place.

Much of the misery we cause ourselves comes from doing things for others we would never do for ourselves.

The secret of getting what you want is not to want it. Next time you desperately want something, try not caring whether you get it. Think back. How many of your sweetest dreams, your greatest desires have come true? On the other hand, how much of what you didn't really care about wound up happening anyway?

Which brings us back to the god of solitude, who also happens to be in charge of denying people what they desperately want. She does it because she believes the more we get what we wish for, the more miserable we'll be, even more so than we already are. How did Truman Capote put it? "More tears are shed for answered prayers than unanswered ones."

The best way to outsmart her, then, is not to care, one way or the other.

Know when to just walk away. It's the key to serenity. After a lifetime of attempting to hold it all together, curmudgeons and solitaires have learned to finally let go. No longer do they anguish over what might have been. No longer do they play the "could've-would've-should've" game. Now they do what they have to, and then they do what they can, and then they turn it over to a higher power, as the addiction recovery folks refer to the act of simply letting go.

"Let it be," the Beatles sang. "Let it be. There will be an answer, let it be." Advice worth repeating. There will always be an answer, regardless of how little or how long we agonize over the question. Why is that so hard to understand when we're young?

If life can't be like the movies, take the movies. If there aren't any more heroes in life to follow, I'll follow the ones in the movies, I've decided.

It's been a long time since someone made me feel like Clark Gable sitting next to Marilyn Monroe in his battered pickup truck in the final scene of the 1961 movie *The Misfits*, the last film that either of them would make. Clark has just turned the wild mustangs loose in the Nevada desert, earning a grateful Marilyn's undying love.

"Where to now?" she asks, voluptuous in blue jeans.

Clark doesn't answer, only points to a bright star in the night sky above the moonlit road curving toward a far horizon.

I'd like to follow their star. Even if it's only in the movies.

Chapter Fourteen

Preparing for the
Trip of a Lifetime

I'm not afraid to die. I just don't
want to be there when it happens.
—Woody Allen

I like to think that he's still alive. That he achieved his goal of seeing one more Christmas, then another, and another. But I doubt it. The last time I saw him he already had beaten the odds for too long. When I called the phone number he gave me five years ago, it had been disconnected. But maybe he only moved, I tell myself. Maybe he's somewhere else by the gray Pacific, still watching the sunsets he loved.

The man I'll call Don Smith was fifty-eight years old on the January morning of 1996 when I visited him on the northern Oregon coast. Expecting to find a frail, wasted victim of the bone cancer he was battling, I was greeted instead by a tall, lean, robust-looking man dressed in an olive sweatshirt, faded jeans, and sturdy hiking boots. Until he told me his age, that he would turn fifty-nine on Valentine's Day, I figured him to be at least ten years younger. How wrong all of my first impressions would be.

On that bleak January day, at a picnic table by the beach, under a pale sun offering light but no warmth, we talked until dark. Rather, he talked and I listened to him tell about living so close to dying, and I eventually filled two notebooks with his words of sorrow, resolution, and regret.

"Don't ever tell someone like me you know how he feels," he said bitterly at one point, "because you can't possibly know until you've lived through it yourself."

Smith learned of his cancer after moving to the coastal town from eastern Oregon on New Year's Day of 1993. By the time the disease was diagnosed, it had ravaged his body for almost two years. His doctor told him he had twelve months more at most.

"That was almost three years ago," Smith said with a wry grin. There had been eight months when the cancer was in remission, but he was back on chemotherapy now. His goal, he said, was to see one more Christmas, still almost a year away.

Hearing Smith describe the ordeals of his cancer was harrowing, but he seemed driven to talk about them, so I listened quietly. Multiple myelomas, the kind in his body, he explained, devour the marrow of bones, rendering them hollow, pitted, and brittle. Since being diagnosed, he had broken and mended some fifty bones.

Just turning over too suddenly in bed, he said, could fracture several ribs. It would take him ten minutes to put on one sock, an hour to get dressed. There were times he had to sleep sitting up in order to breathe, praying the whole time for healing to enter his body. "For a blue light to come from God and carry the cancer away."

He had to ask passersby in the trailer park where he lived to open jar lids for him, to lift cans off supermarket shelves and put them into his cart. He didn't have the strength to pull his trousers together so he could button them and finally devised a method involving a string attached to the doorknob to do the work of his arms.

With all the pain and humiliation he's suffered, he thinks he's paid for his sins—and then some, he said. "I don't think I'll be going to purgatory," Smith added wryly.

At the height of his crippled misery, he lost the will to live, he said. "I felt helpless, useless, each moment of every day consumed with excruciating effort. I agonized over whether to just let go and die." Then the chemotherapy and massive doses of other drugs kicked in. One morning he was able to lift his hands to his piano keyboard and play a few notes of music, and that achievement started him upward again.

Against his doctor's orders not to venture outside the trailer because the bones in his legs might break, not to go out in public because of the risk of infectious diseases, he began attending church once more. Then came the remission, which ended eight months later, but by then the miracles had begun. Not magic, he emphasized, but small *miracles*.

Then he told me something startling: "I know the exact day my cancer started." Smith was quiet for a while as he tried to fight back the only tears I saw him cry the whole time I was with him.

"It happened in eastern Oregon," he went on finally. "I moved there from Iowa with a woman I'd been with after divorcing my wife of twenty-one years." Eastern Oregon, Smith explained, was as similar to Australia as he could find, warm and dry with good fishing, but he would have gone to Australia if he'd been able to qualify for the country's strict immigration quota.

His abrupt severance of the four-year relationship with his "second love," the woman who'd accompanied him to Oregon and whom he had planned to marry, had caused the disease, Smith was convinced. "It was mostly my fault," he said, the anger evident in his voice. "I hurt so bad, I know it triggered the cancer. Within six months after losing her, I began feeling the pain in my bones."

By then, he'd moved to the small seaside community on the Oregon coast. It was there that his cancer was diagnosed. And it was there that the eight months of remission ended—the result, he thought, of an ugly falling-out with a close friend, an engineer also terminally ill, with emphysema.

"That's what brought the cancer back," he said matter-of-factly.

Looking back on the melancholy day we spent together, I understand the truth he was trying to tell me: *We are the sum of our choices.*

The right choices we make result in our goodness and character. The wrong choices harden into bitterness and despair, capable of metastasizing body and soul. And if we don't have the wisdom to make the good choices when we're young, we need the grace to make peace with the bad choices when we're old. So we can die well.

I think that's what Don Smith was trying to do.

Joanne Douglas prefaces her comments on preparing for death with a joke: "The priest asks an elderly parishioner if she's ever thought about the 'hereafter.' The parishioner replies, 'Oh, all the time. I'm always walking into a room, standing there a moment and wondering: What am I here after?'"

That question never really concerned her, says Douglas, sixty-six.

"I was always satisfied with life as it was. Sometimes I looked at women who weren't as encumbered as I was and felt a bit of envy. But just as quickly, I'd think, 'My day is coming.' When I was in college, I felt I could become one of the new career women. Then I became pregnant, married, and the mother of four, but I didn't regret any of it as I always knew, 'My day is coming.'

"I found satisfaction in raising my four kids the best way I knew. I busied myself with PTA, Boy Scouts, Little League. I loved the camping trips, found strength in knowing I could organize and maintain an active household. If I sound like a single parent, technically I wasn't, but with a husband who traveled part of each week, it felt very much to me like being single— until the weekend came and I was no longer in charge."

After the children were in school, Douglas says, she began taking college courses again and later took a job both for the money and the contacts outside of her home.

"When my mother was eighty-two, she suffered illnesses that required much attention. I was an only child, so the obligation fell to me. Also around that time," she went on, "the alcoholism that had been playing around the edges of our marriage began exerting more force in our lives. After much duress, some hysterics, and finally a confrontation, my husband entered a rehab program, and all the while I thought, 'My day will come.'"

She was diagnosed with ovarian cancer four years ago.

Douglas says her surgery was successful, even though the doctors weren't able to remove all the tumors. "Chemotherapy is keeping what's left under control, but the cancer changed my life drastically. I knew I would need to feel in charge of my own life and death," says the mother of three daughters and a son (who have given her four grandchildren to date), who has been married to the same man for forty-three years.

"How am I getting ready for the hereafter?" Douglas gets back to the subject at hand. "By taking care of business," she answers herself.

"By doing the best that I can while I'm still here, by trying to leave with all my i's dotted and t's crossed, so to speak. The job of living isn't over until the final breath is drawn, but the influence of a life is felt long after the last breath. I really believe that. We're all dealing with our mortality," she continues, "though few of us care to admit it, because by admitting death is out there we have to look in the corners and places we might not be ready to face. Confronted with my cancer, I began facing death by getting things done—all the practical considerations my children wouldn't have to handle if I took care of them myself."

These necessary things, then—life's remaining i's to be dotted and t's to be crossed—became the calm acknowledgment of her impending encounter with death.

"When you confront the inevitability of death you realize, consciously or subconsciously, decisions need to be made, things have to be done. Facing up to your mortality—living your life with the awareness it could end long before you fervently hope it will—keeps you from putting off those critical decisions and tasks you'd otherwise 'get around to' someday," Douglas says.

"I need to feel when I leave the house that I've tied everything into as neat a package as I possibly can. Just in case this is the day I don't return. It ranks right up there with my mother's admonition always to wear clean underwear in case I'm in an accident."

And so she started with the place she intends to be buried. "I want a place with a view in a central location—not for me," she adds quickly, "but for friends and relatives who might be induced to drop by and 'share' a glass of wine later." She laughs. "Like the New York mother who wanted to be buried under the parking lot at Saks Fifth Avenue because she knew her daughter would come to visit at least once a week."

With that bit of business taken care of, Douglas says, "I asked myself, 'What else?' Well, there's another necessary player called a funeral home. Certainly this decision could be made by any of my relatives still around, but our family is scattered across the country. Besides, I'd hope, they'll be so devastated by my demise they won't need the extra stress of such decision-making. So I chose to do that for them too."

Douglas laughs again. "One of my daughters saw a shopping bag in my closet marked 'Mom's and Dad's Urns.' Aghast, she asked if that was really what it said. When I explained I wanted them readily accessible, she seemed to understand. It also provided a good opening for me to tell her where my list of wishes and instructions was kept. Which brings us to a service," she continues.

"I've also outlined what I'd like to be done in this regard, which bells and whistles I want and how many. Under stress, people sometimes forget to do things that normally would be second nature to them. So a gentle reminder from mom to the kids to mind their p's and q's and pay all the bills I didn't take care of.

"I've also included suggestions for the kind of going-away party I want after the service, though I probably overstepped the bounds of good taste on this one—no pun intended. Since I haven't ordered the menu from a caterer, they'll probably do whatever they want, and that's all right with me. I just want them to know it's to be a *party*."

Backing up further, Douglas reveals that she has investigated different hospice facilities and nursing homes, listing her acceptable choices in order of preference. Her "Living Trust" is in place as well, stipulating "special bequests" that aren't necessarily of high monetary value but are things she feels will be meaningful to specific children and grandchildren.

"I've also completed a 'Grandmother Remembers' book for each of the grandchildren," she went on. "In addition, the two younger ones will each receive a small chest I'm filling with mementos and letters I've written to them, along with whatever seems important to me at the time. It will be up to the individual parents to decide at what age each child should receive the books and chests. That's not a decision I need to make," she adds.

"I've done all these things because, first, it's my nature to want a say in as much of what involves me as possible. Second, I don't want any decisions made on my behalf in moments of grief and stress that would put undue financial strain on the family budget. By taking care of them myself beforehand, hopefully I'm removing that unnecessary strain."

"Third and most important," Douglas concludes. "I'm doing all these things because they're very important to me at this time of my life. And while I'm doing them, I can speculate on where I'll be when it's all over. Best of all, when the time finally comes, it will make my going that much easier—for myself and for those I love."

"I suppose we've all had thoughts about death, but some of us are faced with that reality much sooner than we'd like," says Zoe Webster, fifty-four, whose breast cancer has reappeared a decade after its initial diagnosis.

Married for ten years in the 1970s, she's now in a relationship that has lasted sixteen years. "So far," Webster adds with a grin. Although she's childless, her partner has a twenty-four-year-old daughter living with them once more. "Just for a few months—or so she says," Webster remarks, displaying her ready humor again.

"We never married because he tried it twice and failed twice," Webster explains, "so this seems to work for both of us. I think it helps us feel we're individuals—independent, yet choosing to be together."

Diagnosed several months ago with a recurrence of her cancer, this time the prognosis is much better, says the freelance graphic designer. "I'm not thinking I'll be dying anytime soon, but ten years ago I was told my chances of surviving were less than 50 percent. Death suddenly became very real to me."

Yet she was greatly surprised at her reaction, Webster says. "I began treatment and found it all quite interesting—uncomfortable, painful at times—but definitely interesting. I learned a great deal about how my body works—and doesn't—and the effect those nasty chemotherapy drugs have on it. I lost my hair and a breast, but not my life," she reveals.

"I suppose I was distracted by the whole process, and even though my death could have been the end result, I found I wasn't afraid at all. And once I realized I wasn't feeling any fear—at least not of dying, only of the pain involved—I was able to reflect on life, and how I felt about mine."

When news of her initial diagnosis reached her friends, Webster says, she was overwhelmed with their good wishes and surrounded by their love. "All of the positive attention was quite heady. The strong connection I suddenly felt to other people convinced me there is one lesson above all to be learned from life. That lesson is love—how to give it and how to receive it. I'm a spiritual person—not to be confused with religious," Webster adds, "but I have no idea what happens after death. Nor do I believe it really matters what any of us believes when the big moment arrives. It is what it is," she says flatly.

"During the time I was so lovingly supported by my friends and family and even some people who barely knew me, I didn't much care what was going to happen, what death would bring or what it wouldn't. I just felt ready to face whatever would come because I'd been so blessed in life."

> "If love is the big lesson of life, then each of us can experience it in its infinite variety, even if we have to give it to ourselves."

Now that she's been rediagnosed with the cancer, she hopes to recapture the calmness and serenity she felt before, Webster concludes. "But I suppose I won't know until it actually happens. My parents were both wonderful role models in dealing with end-of-life issues, and I hope to be able to follow their lead."

I tell Webster she was blessed in having so many loving friends to sustain her. But what if she'd faced death alone, I ask. Does she think she'd have experienced the same calmness and lack of fear?

"I don't know," Webster replies in her candid manner. "But I do know this: If there's no one there to love you, it's absolutely all right to love yourself, to treat *yourself* as a loved one, to provide yourself with the things you'd give to anyone else you loved. If love is the big lesson of life, then each of us can experience it in its infinite variety, even if we have to give it to ourselves."

Webster offers one last thought: "I'm convinced that nearly everyone who's given a gloomy prognosis, who's told life may be coming to an end much sooner than expected, is *changed* by the experience."

"I became determined to live each day as fully as I can. And not to take any of life too seriously. I find I have less patience now doing things I find boring. Or spending time with people I don't especially like. Time is such a strange thing—it flies by whether or not you're having fun.

"So I choose to have fun!"

For most of us, however, enjoying life means disavowing its natural conclusion. A May 2000 survey sponsored by the National Hospice Foundation confirmed that death is still a word that sticks in our throats.

More than a quarter of the 1,250 American adults forty years of age and older interviewed in the study indicated that they weren't likely to discuss a parent's impending death with that parent. The result is that the needs of the dying—and those they leave behind—often go unmet.

It's a problem, notes foundation president Karen Davie, that will only increase unless a change of attitude is effected over the next thirty years, during which time the number of U.S. seniors will double from nearly forty million to almost eighty million.

Fewer than 25 percent of Americans have put into writing how they'd like to be cared for when they die, and only 36 percent have talked to someone about their wishes, the National Hospice Foundation survey revealed. Around half said they'd rely on family or friends to make end-of-life decisions for them, but many hadn't talked to anyone about their desires.

Another finding: while 18 percent of the respondents indicated they weren't likely to discuss safe sex with their children, 28 percent said they probably wouldn't bring up the impending death of their parents with their children.

"We have a long history of avoiding the subject," affirms Greg Palmer, author of *Death: The Trip of a Lifetime* and producer of the PBS series by the same name.

On February 20, 2000, Carly Ames, forty-five, kissed her husband of fifteen years good-bye as he departed their home in Tennessee, bound for Texas in his eighteen-wheeler. On May 1, she received a phone call from the state police that his company had reported the long-haul trucker missing. Two days later, she received another call informing her that her husband had been found in his rig, parked off a highway in Texas. Barely forty-eight, he had died of a heart attack.

"I guess I'm too soon into widowhood to tell you how magnificent it is to be alone," Ames said in anguish three weeks later. "I'm in a nightmare I can't wake from," she wrote in the first of a series of E-mail conversations that took place between us after her heartrending loss. "I just started looking on the Internet for anything—anybody I could talk to about my pain. I can't stand the pain. I just want to curl up in a corner somewhere and wait to die. But it helps me to write about it, and so I do."

I wrote back telling her that there was nothing I could say, of course, to ease her pain, but that I thought she was doing the right thing in embracing her grief, terrible as it might be. My father had died suddenly when I was young, I told her, so I felt a special empathy for what she must be going through, that no one had helped me or my sister or our three brothers address our own loss, that I waited almost a lifetime to broach the pent-up sorrow, that by finally allowing myself to mourn I came to understand how important it is to acknowledge our sorrow, and by so doing I finally found the closure that I should have had as a boy.

"I know I'm not the only one who's experienced great loss," she wrote back. "But I just feel so cheated right now. At least I have a little comfort in knowing my husband had lain down in the bunk of his long-haul truck—his home away from home—to sleep as he did every night. A while ago I fussed at him for smoking and told him that if he got lung cancer and died the horrible death my father did two years ago, I was going to shoot him.

"He just smiled at me and said, 'I'm not going to die of lung cancer. I'm going to close my eyes and go to sleep like my dad did.' Of course, his dad was seventy and Bob was forty-eight. I'm sure he didn't think he was facing death."

Ames went on to tell about the "big bear of a man with a heart of gold who bounded into my life and changed it forever." Divorced at thirty with a four-year-old daughter, she had sworn she would never remarry.

"He took one look at me and saw how scared I was to commit to someone again, and he said, 'Trust me. It's OK, trust me.' And it was. He always told everyone it was a 'package deal—a wife and a kid.' He became a real father to my little girl, who's now nineteen. The other day, when my mom told her not to forget her 'real daddy,' my daughter said, 'I have a biological father. I lost my real daddy.' So here we are," Ames wrote, "me, my mom, and my daughter—big gaping wounds from having our hearts ripped out."

Aside from talking to a therapist, she has found some solace with "a group of people all in the same pain as me. If you want to talk, you talk; if you want to cry, you cry; and no one says, 'Oh, I'm so sorry, I didn't mean to upset you—don't cry, you'll mess your face up.' There's one thing I've found out—

people you work with are not comfortable with you expressing grief. They want to put you on *their* timeline. They think that because time has gone by and they aren't thinking about their losses, that you shouldn't be thinking about yours. I *hate* that," Ames said.

"I've learned a valuable lesson from this—that from now on, when I meet a relative or close friend who's lost someone, the nicest thing I can do is put my arms around them and just say, 'I'm so sorry.' That's all. That's enough. None of that 'God knows best' stuff, which may be true but isn't something you need to hear in the first few weeks.

"No 'Well, at least you had him for fifteen years.' So what? I wanted him for fifteen more. I wasn't ready to give him up!

"No 'He wouldn't want you to grieve for him.' That's bull crap."

I asked Ames what she thought she had to do to get through this terrible time. "You sound like a strong person," I wrote back, "someone whose survival instincts are worth listening to. Even though you're still struggling with your pain, still groping for some answers, what do you think you have to do to help yourself cope and survive?"

A week went by with no word. Then, on June 16, a month and a day after she'd learned her husband had died, Ames wrote for the last time. "I guess you noticed I didn't readily come back to you," she said. "Those were hard questions you asked me to answer—what I have to do to survive, to cope, and most days I feel I'm not. But I know that isn't true because most days I'm able to get out of bed and, with the grace of God, report to work on time, even though I've walked the floors for two hours of the night and begged for sleep to come," she revealed.

"You're right, though, in that I *am* a survivor. My first marriage was not a success and I survived by getting up every day and saying to myself, 'I am not going to let this beat me!' So that is what I do now when it would be easy to curl up in a corner and say, 'I am totally shutting down—I am not going to deal with this right now and will just be Jell-O.'

"And then this strong inner self I thought had left me rises up and says, 'Yes, you're going to work today. And you're going to hold your head up high and walk through that door, past the glances filled with pity, past the whispers, to your desk and go to work.' Somehow I've found the strength to do so.

"No, I don't talk to the same people. I don't gather at the coffee pot and laugh and make jokes and tell the funny things Rob did the past weekend. But I *am* at work, trying to be productive, and that is all I can do right now.

"I only want to be with my real friends right now, people who I know I am safe with, who care about me and don't want to know all the sordid details of my nightmare so they can run and repeat it to the office gossipers down the hall. I've developed a paranoia you wouldn't believe.

"I've only been to the coffee store twice in all this time (when I used to go once or twice a week). There are no groceries in the house, and I'm out of everything else as well, but I can't stand to go to large places because I always see someone who knows me and knows my story and I'll see them looking at me from a distance. They don't approach me, just stand staring, and I can't handle it right now.

"So that is my survival technique—either spending quality time alone with my memories or going to friends for supper, taking walks around a nearby lake, or talking on the phone to people I know and trust. Yes, it's a lonely existence, but it's all I have to cling to. I have a daughter to finish raising, and I have to think of her.

"Everyone says it will get better, time will heal the wound. Well, I'm still waiting for that day. It isn't here, and I don't think it will be for a long time.

"Meanwhile, I find comfort in my faith in God, in the wonderful family and friends He's placed in my path. On my lowest days, something will happen that lets me know He's watching out for me, that He sends just the right person to minister to me and to comfort my heart when I need it most."

On those rare occasions when we actually ponder death, the tendency is to view the inevitable occasion as a postponable encounter with a formidable but gullible pest. As implacable, for instance, as death appears in Ingmar Bergman's classic film, *The Seventh Seal*, the king of terrors is nonetheless diverted from his morbid mission, if only for a while. The knight he has come for challenges him to a game of chess. They play.

The knight loses and he, his squire, and their friends die. But death is later tricked into sparing the lives of a family of roving actors.

When the somber figure comes for Nat Ackerman in Woody Allen's one-act play, *Death Knocks*, Ackerman cajoles him into a game of gin rummy. To Ackerman's delight, death turns out to be a comical patsy who winds up losing $28 and vows to return the next day for another game to win back his money.

"Anything you want," Ackerman replies. "Double or nothing we'll play. I'm liable to win an extra week or a month. The way you play, maybe years." On his way out, death trips on a hall rug and takes a pratfall down the stairs.

The play ends with Ackerman phoning a friend to inform him gleefully, "Moe, he's such a *schlep!*"

Ah, Woody, if only he were.

Still, it's comforting to regard death as an amiable bumbler we can con indefinitely, even if our denial gets harder with every passing year—and each loved one who passes on. And so I've quit trying to get that grim ferryman out of my mind whenever he paddles into my consciousness.

Not that I care to hasten his arrival, mind you. Physically, through sensible nutrition and exercise, I'm trying to live forever. But mentally and emotionally, I'm preparing to die. The more I practice, I figure, the better I'll be at it when the time comes.

Another reason I no longer try to avoid the subject is simply because I can't. Solitaires have a hard time doing that. Spend enough time alone and you'll find that facing death becomes as inevitable as confronting denial. With so much time to think and nowhere to hide, I've simply quit trying.

What's more, as the omega moment draws nearer, while I wait and ponder—no longer its inevitability, but its imminence—how I handle my growing awareness of that premier event has become paramount to my emotional well-being.

When the grim reaper finally said howdy to George Burns, America's beloved entertainer had no parting gags. No matter. The eldest statesman of comedy had fired off enough one-liners about dying to prepare himself well for his last curtain call.

"He often said he knew entrances and exits," a longtime friend told mourners. "Last Saturday he knew it was time to go."

Joking about the trip isn't a bad way to get ready for it. Neither is living to be a hundred years and forty-nine days, as Burns did, having his cake and cigar too, while laughing all the way.

"To go out into solitude, to go out into the desert night," John Dunne assures us, "is to meet the fear head-on. It is to make love with what one fears.... It is to enter into a love that casts out fear."

Make love, not war, then, with that ashen king of terrors, for he rides a fast camel, as an ancient Arab proverb reminds us.

Why not just ignore him until he sidles up? For two good reasons, one having to do with dying a good death, the other with living a good life, and both inextricably joined.

Staring death in the eye keeps us squarely in the present. It makes us question our priorities, pushes us into doing things we might otherwise put off. It turns the pessimistic phrase, "Life is short!" into a rallying cry for maximum effort and sustained passion in the time remaining to each of us.

Not that I propose sitting around, contemplating how it feels not to exist. For one thing, it's impossible to imagine. Your ego simply won't permit it. "The world without *me*? Unthinkable!" Try it—all you'll do is give yourself a headache. Take my word for it. But if accepting the naturalness, the inevitability, even the imminence of death, keeps us from wasting life, this is a better thing, no?

Buddhist monk Sogyal Rinpoche put it this way: "Perhaps it is only those who understand just how fragile life is who know how precious it is."

None of this, of course, applies to the young. There's nothing so tragic as a death before it's time, no sorrow as unbearable as outliving one's child. For the young, as Andy Rooney once suggested, death is a distant rumor—and should remain that way for as long as possible. All things in their own time, as the Bible tells us.

Better that the young put their attention, ardor, energy, and hope into living life rather than contemplating death.

But reading a newspaper account of one young woman's fatal accident on a midsummer morning a few years ago got me thinking about how I'd have liked to have departed before my time if that had been my destiny. If I'd had to die young, I decided, hers is the death I would have chosen.

She was twenty-two, the story disclosed—bright, talented, beautiful, her future spread before her like a brilliant, textured tapestry. She'd just graduated from a prestigious eastern university, had accepted a communications position with a New York television network, and would depart the following day on a four-week holiday in Europe before embarking on her promising career and the rest of her exciting life.

On that golden summer day, the young woman had just finished her morning run. She had sprinted the last half mile, then stopped abruptly to catch her breath. She was bent at the waist, hands on her knees, eyes on the ground, her mind a world away, perhaps in Barcelona or Tuscany or Rome, exulting in the enchanting sights she would see, the splendid life she would have; it was then that the train hit her.

Unaware, unthinking, oblivious to everything but the beguiling visions in her head, she had ended her run on the railroad tracks that wound through the center of her small Oregon town—one moment in the fullest expectancy of her glorious youth, adrenaline and endorphins coursing through her body, sugarplum visions dancing in her head; the next moment, gone, the transition instantaneous, irrevocable, and complete.

But now that I'm old, I've decided how I want to go. Even though I know we all die alone, regardless of how many loved ones we gather around us, when the time comes I'd like to be part of that hilarious stateroom scene in the classic Marx Brothers comedy *A Night at the Opera*.

The scene would unfold exactly as it does in the movie. The same ship's steward would wrestle the identical steamer trunk into Groucho's minuscule cabin aboard the *SS Americus*. From the trunk would emerge the three stowaways: Chico, Harpo, and their baritone friend, Allan Jones. Then, one by one, shoehorning themselves into the diminutive room would come the two chambermaids, followed by the small engineer with a huge wrench, then the manicurist—who asks Groucho whether he wants his nails long or short, to which Groucho replies, "Better make them short, it's getting crowded in here"—then the engineer's massive assistant with a tiny wrench, then the young woman in search of her lost Aunt Minnie, then the burly maid with her mop and bucket, and finally the three stewards balancing precarious breakfast trays.

When the indomitable Mrs. Claypoole finally knocks on the stateroom door and Groucho opens it, an avalanche of arms and legs will engulf her, exactly as in the movie. Before then, however, Death, preferably in the gossamer-white guise of Jessica Lange (as she portrayed the not grim but gorgeous reaper in the 1979 movie *All That Jazz*), will have slipped in and found me, happy and oblivious in the tangle of bodies and Groucho's banter and the playful honks of Harpo's squeezehorn.

And what happens afterwards? Well, I'm still working on that. For one thing, I've started picturing God as the kindly, loving patriarch I now believe him to be—much, in fact, like George Burns as he appeared in the 1977 movie, *Oh, God!*, in a plaid shirt, tan trousers, baseball cap, and comfortable walking shoes, viewing the world bemusedly through horn-rimmed glasses.

For most of my life, you see, I pictured God the way artists have portrayed Him through the centuries: harsh and austere with wild white hair and an angry white beard, his countenance stern and vengeful, a stark reminder that my immortal soul hung above the eternal abyss whenever I had the temerity to cross Him.

I also think now that He sends very few people to hell. Not so when I was young. Back then, Roman Catholics could go to hell for just about anything: missing mass on Sunday, eating meat on Friday, receiving communion in the state of mortal sin, masturbating—you name it, you could jeopardize your immortal soul doing it. Even committing an act you *thought* was a mortal sin made it so, even if it really wasn't.

The catch-22 catechism of my childhood contained illustrations of souls whose mortal sins—sketched as dark blotches within the outline of a lily-white heart—teetered them on the brink of damnation. Venial sins, which weren't soul threatening but did lengthen one's time in the cleansing fires of purgatory, were indicated by smaller splatters. And hearts drawn with no offensive blemishes represented sinners rendered pure by the redemptive sacrament of confession, ready to enter—if not heaven, at least purgatory.

Fearing God as greatly as I did in my hell-and-brimstone Catholic youth, I wound up praying to someone far less intimidating: a person named Mary, the warm, compassionate mother of Jesus, a gentle, loving, infinitely more approachable figure than the Heavenly Father. So when I prayed, it was always to sweet Mary, "Our Mother, who art in heaven ..."

But as the time draws closer for that celestial confrontation, it seems to me I ought to start conversing with God directly. It's why I've begun painting a benign and amiable, even comical face on the creator I used to dread, someone who'd laugh uproariously at the suggestion of casting people into hell for masturbating. It's my way of making Him more user-friendly.

And because we all hold in our hearts our own special impression of the Supreme Being, because there are no rules, no limits on how we can perceive or experience Him, each of us sees God in a different way, in different things: drifting clouds, ocean sunsets, the purity of a child. And each of us is right, I've decided. No one way is better than another. All that matters is that we *want* to experience Him as often as possible, whatever it takes.

Which is why in my heaven, God is a geezer who resembles George Burns, and doesn't mind a bit.

Sometimes you have to lose something precious to gain something just as dear. For Linda Josephson, it took nearly dying to realize that she needed to *live*—in the truest sense of the word.

"We miss so much and limit ourselves so greatly by not being open to all that's good and positive in our existence," says the fifty-three-year-old wife, mother, and business owner. All that changed ten years ago when she was diagnosed with stage-four lymphoma. Josephson had just turned forty-four.

"Cancer doesn't run on my side of the family," she reveals. "I've always lived a healthy, active, squeaky-clean life. But after five months of treatment for what my doctor thought was a kidney infection, and a lower-back problem that wasn't getting any better with chiropractic care and bed rest, I told my husband the constant, severe pain was taking away my will to live.

Knowing how much I love life and all the reasons I have to live, he rushed me to the hospital on March 8, 1990."

At the medical center, extensive tests and biopsies revealed the virulent cancer. Josephson was told that an aggressive mass of malignant cells had invaded her glands, bones, bone marrow, and body fluids, was pushing into her spinal cord, had collapsed three of her vertebrae, and would soon enter her brain. Furthermore, she was experiencing nerve damage, had grown acutely anemic, and was rapidly losing body weight and mass.

Looking up at the team of physicians standing at her bedside on that first fateful morning, Josephson made three resolutions. Though she felt that death was near, she would trust the team of doctors dedicated to her recovery and open herself fully to all of the treatment options. She would absorb every bit of strength and encouragement that came her way. And she would fight for her life with every fiber of her being.

"I was reduced to taking mere moments of time and clinging to anything remotely positive," she says.

"My body and my life were out of control. All I could do was pray for strength and grace. I never want to forget the depth of my need in those utterly helpless moments. I never want to forget the unconditional, limit-less help given to me to regain control of my health. I never want to lose the level of awareness the cancer granted me, and the clear perspective of what life is all about.

"As I lay in bed and let others care for me, I felt flooded with love and appreciation. As I reflected on death, forgiveness was foremost in my mind. I began to let go of darkness and move toward light. I felt strangely confident. I calmly planned my funeral. Then I planned to *live*."

It turns out that she needed every ounce of courage and resolve she could muster, Josephson says. In the harrowing months that followed, there were endless exams, X-rays, medications, blood transfusions, CT scans, MRIs, and finally two surgeries followed by aggressive chemotherapy treatments.

Before the initial treatment, she had what she calls her "Red Rain" vision.

"To this day," she says, "its hope and promise comfort me."

When the cancer was found, and Josephson was given a short time to live without intensive treatment, she began using visualization methods to help fight the disease, she reveals. The healing vision came soon after.

"Lying in my hospital bed," Josephson says, "I closed my eyes and a vivid picture appeared before me. When I opened my eyes, the picture was still clear and evident. There was a beautiful blue sky with white fluffy clouds floating aimlessly. Quickly, though, the clouds became dark and angry, fighting for position in the sky. Soon the whole sky was black and violent and torrents of rain pelted down. Gradually this intense rain began to turn crimson in color. In time the red rain let up and turned to crystal snowflakes that floated down and dissipated. The sky became clear again, sunny and warm with a rosy glow. It was like a lingering sunset that captivated my whole being."

The white clouds that turned dark and violent represent her immunity cells invaded by the cancer, Josephson explains. The crimson rain represents her life-giving red blood cells, empowered by chemotherapy, that wash away the cancer. The reemerging sun and clear skies represent her cancer-free cells restored to energy and health.

But other analogies come to mind, she says. "The black clouds might signify the need for healing. The red rain could symbolize the blood of Christ and the critical importance of forgiveness and spiritual cleansing in our lives. The crystal snowflakes could denote the purity and truth that follow forgiveness, with the sun and warmth embodying the love and blessings that become free-flowing."

"I firmly believe," she adds, "that renewed health also means the restoration of mind, soul, and spirit as well as body."

In remission now for nearly ten years, she credits her cure to modern medicine, intense prayer, an enduring faith, and the purifying vision of red rain that turned dark clouds into crystal snowflakes.

But Josephson has learned much more from her ordeal—lessons, she says, that will last the rest of her life, however long.

One of these lessons is never to lose the level of awareness and the clear perspective that her wake-up call provided her. "I couldn't change my frightening situation," she concludes, "but I could change my attitude toward it. I came to realize that fear, rather than paralyzing a person, can serve as a passageway to true faith."

"In my deep soul-searching as I faced death, love and forgiveness kept coming up as the all-important things in life. Love and forgiveness equal compassion. And if compassion guides our words and actions, we will always be moving toward the light, in the direction of all that is good and honorable in our existence." But cancer doesn't end with remission or a cure.

"There are side effects and issues that remain. The desperateness of the disease stays with us and makes us aware of the feelings we need to deal with in order to maintain our overall health. Mental and emotional healing take longer than physical healing, and we may not have as much help with that process.

"I feel eventually we're meant to share the simple truths with which our cancer experience has blessed us. One of the greatest of these truths is that fear doesn't have to paralyze us. If we take it on ourselves to move past that fear, to summon our courage to do for ourselves what no one else can do for us, it can serve as a passageway to limitless faith, hope, forgiveness, and a liberated, love-motivated future."

"With remission, we're given more time, a second chance," she adds. "With my altered perspective, I'm learning to allow myself to be the 'real' me rather than the 'super' me. Somewhere in my development as a person, my true self was often denied or squelched, creating a false and idealized self. Cancer gave me the awareness that I was stifled, suffocating, maybe living a lie. I began using my energies for honest growth rather than the maintenance of my approval-seeking self. I'm now in the process of freeing myself from my condemnation to that place between what I really am and what I was trying to be. This condemnation, in itself, is a form of cancer."

Pronounced cured of her lymphoma ten years after its diagnosis, she's considered a true survivor by her family and friends, Josephson says. And now that she's been restored to health and a state of wholeness, it's important for her to help others understand the true nature of loneliness, weakness, grace, and strength.

"My own survival prayer was for courage and grace to face the unknown, and I received it." This, she says, was the greatest gift her ordeal with cancer gave her, a life-affirming realization in the form of a paradox that she will hold close forever: "Once you reach total solitude in the experience of facing death, you find we are not alone in the end."

We all must look *inside* ourselves for the faith, courage, and hope we need to bear the omega moment of our lives. When we turn to ourselves, we reconcile our greatest fear—that each of us must die alone.

———————

I once asked a venerable old doctor what he told his patients as they were dying.

"I tell them what they want to hear," the doctor replied.

"If they're religious, I tell them they're going to heaven. If they're not, I tell them they led a good life and that's all that matters. I tell them whatever they want to hear."

I remember being disappointed by his answer, thinking him flip and callous. Now I realize that he was wise and compassionate.

For we need to believe our own truths, not someone else's, particularly when we are dying. We need to know that what's in our heart is *right*.

And if no one is there to tell us what we desperately want to hear, then we have to tell it to ourselves.

Chapter Fifteen

The Long, Courageous
Journey to Ourselves

Alone on a wide, wide sea.
—Samuel Taylor Coleridge

In the waning days of 1991, Paul Theroux's literary agent asked him which French personality he would most like to meet; "d'Aboville," the author replied.

"He is my hero," Theroux told Gerard d'Aboville's wife Cornelia when the two were introduced soon after. "Mine, too," she replied.

"And mine," millions around the world would have echoed warmly, myself included.

A decade later, though, most people have to be reminded that d'Aboville was the forty-seven-year-old Frenchman who rowed across the Pacific Ocean alone in his 26' boat, *Sector*. Paddling ten to twelve hours per day, he battled hundred-mile-per-hour winds, and towering waves that capsized his boat more than thirty times during the crossing, once trapping him upside-down in his hermetic cabin for nearly two hours before he managed to right the boat again. Then he kept on rowing.

"Endurance for one moment more" is how men of the Caucasus Mountains define heroism. One moment more. For as long as it takes. When the moments are endured alone, the act exceeds heroism, extending into unimaginable courage and glory.

On the evening of November 21, 1991, 134 grueling days after leaving Choshi, Japan, weighing thirty-seven pounds less than when he embarked on his impossible journey, d'Aboville stepped ashore at the port of Ilwaco, a fishing village fourteen miles from where I now live on Washington's North Beach Peninsula.

I remember my excitement, driving with two friends from Portland to Astoria, Oregon, on that frigid November morning, hoping for a glimpse of the heroic figure who had captured the world's imagination with his solo conquest of the mighty Pacific. D'Aboville had already departed by the time we arrived, but the anticipation of seeing such a man made the trip worthwhile.

"Why," English explorer Apsley Cherry-Garrard asked himself on one of his own solitary adventures, "do some human beings desire with such urgency to do such things, regardless of the consequences, voluntarily, conscripted by no one but themselves?" Theroux asked the same question of d'Aboville when the two men finally met.

"Only an animal does useful things," d'Aboville answered. "An animal gets food, finds a place to sleep, tries to keep comfortable. But I wanted to do something that was not useful—not like an animal at all. Something only a human being would do."

And do alone, if only to achieve that rare benediction bestowed singly on those who dare brave incredible hardships with only their reserves of courage and spirit to sustain them.

In 1933, with his Antarctic expedition bivouacked between Little America and the South Pole, Admiral Richard E. Byrd decided to spend the winter alone at the Bolling Advance Weather Base. "Now, I wanted something more than just privacy in the geographical sense," Byrd later wrote in his book, *Alone*.

"Out there in the South Polar barrier, in cold and darkness as complete as that of the Pleistocene, I should have time to catch up, to study and think and listen to the phonograph; and, for maybe seven months, remote from all but the simplest distractions, I should be able to live exactly as I chose, obedient to no necessities but those imposed by wind and night and cold, and to no man's laws but my own."

In his own book, *Seul* (French for "alone"), written in 1992 about his Pacific crossing, d'Aboville explains why he attempted such a desolating excursion. Ten days after setting off from Choshi, Japan, in ideal weather with a brisk wind at his back and the churning terrors of 40' troughs still ahead, he enjoyed one of his most successful days, rowing twelve hours and covering thirty knots toward his distant destination. That evening, d'Aboville wrote in his journal:

> "I am a resistance fighter in a war I invented for myself. The enemy is me, with all my physical shortcomings, my temptation to give up. That temptation, by the way, does not consist of sending up my distress signal and throwing in the towel, as one might think.
>
> "It is the thousand and one little daily temptations that lie in wait for us all: to get out of bed five minutes later than usual; to stop one minute before the bell rings signaling the end of the working day; to pull a trifle less vigorously on the oar next time; even to stop shaving.
>
> "These are the kinds of minor abandonments, the easings off just a little here and there, which in and of themselves are insignificant but which, taken together, ineluctably lead to the ultimate surrender. And it is these same minor, ridiculous battles, these repetitive, fastidious, inglorious battles that, if I persist, will eventually lead me to victory."

Robert Bogucki decided he needed to isolate himself for a long period of time. He chose to do it beginning on July 12, 1999, in Australia's Great Sandy Desert. After telling a friend that he planned to rely solely on his spiritual resources during his four-hundred-mile trek through the desert, the thirty-three-year-old volunteer fireman from Fairbanks, Alaska, disappeared into the brutally inhospitable terrain, setting off a massive search that was subsequently depicted in an hour-long segment of *Dateline NBC*.

Rescuers who followed Bogucki deep into the 160,000-square-mile wasteland—terrain so harsh even Aborigines don't live there—marveled at how he was able to keep going for so long. They knew he couldn't possibly carry enough food and water to sustain him the whole way, and with every 90-degree day that passed, hope dimmed for the man the Australian media had dubbed "the desert vagabond."

Finally, after several hundred miles, his footsteps disappeared. The search was officially declared at an end. Bogucki's parents, however, hired a professional team to sustain the effort. Trackers and dogs in trucks and helicopters were deployed and miraculously picked up his trail again. Then they found his camping gear.

By then he'd been alone in the desert for six weeks with no known supplies. Searchers in a helicopter finally came across his backpack, tarpaulin, water bottle, and his most-prized possession—the Bible he was never without. And the tracks leading on, resolutely straight until now, seemed confused. Also, his footfalls weren't as strong, and his rest periods came much too often.

Where initially he had averaged twenty-five miles a day, he was now covering less than three. What's more, revealed the *Dateline* narrator, Bogucki's girlfriend had disclosed his intention, if he decided that he wasn't going to make it, to secrete himself somewhere in the vast wilderness to die. Then, with the hope of finding him dwindling with each passing hour, the searchers suddenly came across him, "just strolling along, head down, oblivious to the roar of the helicopter," according to one rescuer.

Weak, gaunt, his skin hanging loosely on a now-skeletal frame, Bogucki was flown to a nearby hospital. He had lost forty-four pounds, roughly a third of his former body weight. Otherwise, he was fine.

Meanwhile, people around the world were asking, "Is the man crazy?" "Why did he do such a thing?" "What was he looking for, anyway?" Bogucki's answers came four months later in a filmed interview. He said he'd dreamed of making such a journey for ten years, that he did it because he needed to know that God exists, otherwise his life would be pointless.

He had originally planned to ride his bicycle across the desert, he said, but the terrain was so sandy that walking was easier. As his strength withered he forced himself to keep going, felt he'd eventually come to the place where he'd be "tested." He once went three days without water, got desperate and dug six feet with his bare hands and found water. He ate desert flowers.

As he walked, he spent the time thinking, he said, thinking and crying. He thought of his life; how much love God has for people. And he kept walking. He walked for weeks with no food to sustain him and barely any water.

He tried not to lose his mind, he said, and had left the Bible behind because he didn't need it anymore.

Then he spelled out "HELP" with rocks on a stretch of open ground. And he kept walking. "Ready to die, at peace," he said later.

Bogucki found water barely minutes before the helicopter came upon him—forty days after he'd set out into the desert. He had walked 240 miles without food, surviving by eating plants and flowers and drinking muddy water. The number forty was no coincidence, he claimed, because both God and Moses were in the desert exactly forty days. "God did that," he said.

The most important thing to him, Bogucki disclosed at the end of the *Dateline* interview, was that he'd found his relationship to God. He also said that he had married his girlfriend of the past eleven years, that he'd become more of the person he wanted to be and could be close to someone else now, and that he didn't need to go without food and water to find God anymore.

"Better," he said, "to show compassion and kindness."

Gerard d'Aboville is a hero for everyone whose unspectacular successes rely on a modicum of inspiration and a maximum of effort, particularly for those who have only themselves to count on.

People such as d'Aboville—those rare, indomitable men and women who set off alone to transcend incredible hardships and danger—awe us with the same dread and fascination that we hold for solitude.

Why do they *do* it? And why *alone*? It's one thing to be tagged by destiny to survive a solitary ordeal. Choosing it is another.

Steven Callahan, a naval architect cast adrift for seventy-six days on a 5-1/2' inflatable raft in the Atlantic, weathered mental, physical, and psychological challenges equal to d'Aboville's. But disaster survivors such as Callahan are spared the doubt, second-guessing, and self-recrimination that perhaps bedevil solo adventurers in their darkest hours, for the latter have no one to blame but themselves, not even fate, for thrusting them in harm's way.

Why, then, do men and women such as d'Aboville embark on their perilous journeys alone? Why is single-handedness such a crucial element of their exploits? Would their psychic rewards be diminished—or different somehow—if they shared their adventures with others?

I searched for answers in d'Aboville's book. I found it interesting that, to the Frenchman, the most significant aspect of his incredible feat was that he had accomplished it alone (and thus had titled his book *Seul*).

Searching the text for words that might divulge his feelings about the need to test himself utterly alone, the closest thing to an explanation I found came in a notation he made after his fantastic voyage:

"When I set out from Choshi, my goal had not been altruistic. I'm not a guru by any means. I have no message to deliver. No light to shine upon the world. And yet, as I read on, day after day [the letters he received after his adventure], I realized that despite myself I had given hope to all kinds of people: prisoners, the unemployed, the downtrodden, the homeless. I had touched the lives of people who, for whatever reason, were depressed and discouraged.

"And, I also saw, I had brought a ray of hope and sunshine into the lives of the aged, those who so often were, as I had been, distressingly alone."

The azure day had slipped away. The sun was about to plunge its crimson glow into the Pacific as I asked Don Smith what he regretted most about dying at the age of fifty-eight.

"The nervous years," replied the man from Idaho, fighting to stay alive on the Oregon coast. He had used the words once before in telling me about his life before the onslaught of cancer. I asked him what he was like back then, in the "nervous" years.

"Controlling," he answered abruptly, almost irritably, as if the memory pained him.

"I was self-centered, constantly competitive, totally driven. My egocentric characteristics dominated my life. I felt I could talk anyone under the table, overwhelm them with my experiences, and I tried every chance I got.

"I was always trying to prove my worth, usually at the expense of those closest to me. I always had to show how dynamic, how talented, how fascinating, and successful I was. I know the need came from a lack of belief in myself. Because I didn't have it, I had to get it from others."

Smith was becoming angry now, not at me, I sensed, but at himself for the waste of all those driven years. His voice had been sad when he talked about the wife he divorced after twenty-one years, and their two sons and a daughter now in their thirties and living in different parts of the country. He hadn't seen any of them in close to eight years.

"I didn't support or comfort her," he said of their mother. "All she needed was approval from me. It's my most terrible regret, never having told her she was doing good—only bad, always the bad."

Smith laughed humorlessly. "I suffered from migraine headaches my whole life," he said, "and now that I'm dying they've gone away along with the colon ulcers I used to get." He shook his head. "That was the only good that came from all the bad."

Time was short now. I told him I needed to get started on my long drive home. "What have you learned from living so close to dying these past few years?" I asked him finally. "What would you say to help others make their lives and deaths better?"

This is what he told me in our last few minutes together:

"Learn to forgive. First others, then yourself—mostly yourself. But you *have* to forgive.

"Get rid of the negativity. So much of your life can go down this dark drain if you let it. Every negative feeling makes you sicker. Every positive feeling makes you better.

"Take life one day at a time. It's good advice, believe me. I go one better now—I take it one minute at a time, one second at a time. Every moment of life is precious.

"Cherish your health while you have it. A few years ago, my closest friend was diagnosed with cancer and heart disease from smoking. He'd been told many years ago to quit. At the time I said I was going to quit too, but I didn't and neither did he. Now I have extreme disdain for people with intelligence who deliberately poison themselves when everything I do is desperately aimed at keeping myself alive.

"Write down all the things you want to do and do the best thing first. You can wind up doing nothing if all you do is consider the possibilities. So just concentrate on one thing—and *do* it. Then move on to the next.

"Be grateful for what you have, for one good reason: You may not have it much longer. Trust me on this.

"Enjoy life! So much becomes unimportant when you're dying. Don't live in denial about death. It really *won't* happen to somebody else—to everyone but you.

"Make peace with yourself. It's wonderful to feel you no longer have to dominate everyone and everything in your life. It's such a relief not trying to be the constant center of your universe.

"Believe in something other than yourself: God, Buddha, the pyramids, whatever will help your internal healing and growth.

"Accept the reality that is you and work from there. Don't fool yourself with false hope. If you do, it will be more painful in the end.

"Get the clutter out of your life. Keep only what's important and concentrate on it fully.

"Don't give up. If you can be useful to yourself and helpful to others, that's enough reason for living."

I thanked Don Smith and said good-bye. I never saw him again. I hope he's still somewhere beside the Pacific, watching the sunsets he loved. I hope the man from Iowa, facing death alone by the sea, has become the hero he was meant to be.

Seven years after moving to the beach—lock, stock, barrel, fax, modem, computer, and WordPerfect—I've begun a tally of what I know about solitude.

I've learned, for one thing, that it's best taken in large doses, as anyone knows who's tried to shake an addiction, be it drugs, alcohol, food, gambling, sex—or people. A jealous mistress, solitude demands but gratefully rewards uncompromising devotion.

I've come to believe that there's an overworked, undervalued god of solitude up there, relatively low in the divine pecking order, with a full and varied job description that includes making sure whatever goes around comes around.

She's also in charge of rewarding risk and commitment: giving everyone exactly what they deserve, even though she usually takes her sweet time about doing it because she's so busy. It's because of her that the guy who won't quit his day job never achieves his dream. She's why nothing of real value happens to us until we believe in ourselves.

What the god of solitude teaches is that anything not worth the risk is not worth attaining. That the greater the gamble, the dearer the prize. That failure, loss, and rejection won't kill you, but not trying surely will, because it breeds regret, and enough regrets are lethal.

It's because of her that I've learned to ask myself, "Who are you trying to impress anyway?" And to hear my exultant reply, "Not a blessed soul!"

But myself, of course.

It's because of her that I'm finally in a time and place where my self-affirmation, my self-fulfillment, my self-esteem have little to do with what other people think of me and everything to do with what I think of myself.

How sad, the god of solitude teaches, that we spend our entire lives auditioning for others—parents, teachers, employers, suitors, spouses, lovers, strangers, friends—only to realize that we should have put ourselves at the head of the line, earned our own love, respect,

> "What the god of solitude teaches is that anything not worth the risk is not worth attaining."

and affection first. And everything else would have taken care of itself.

How tragic, she whispers mournfully, that we wait so long to free ourselves from other people's expectations, to find our true worth in our own eyes instead of in the eyes of others.

Look in the mirror, the god of solitude teaches. You will see the only eyes that matter, the only eyes that truly appreciate and understand you. In them, you will find all the respect and approval, all the love and esteem that you desire.

Then everything you receive from others will come as a gift, not a need.

And you will know, at last, that far from the price, solitude is the prize that time alone can give you.

Bibliography

Allen, Woody. *The Complete Prose of Woody Allen*. New York: Wing Books, 1991.

American Psychiatric Association. *Diagnostic and Statistical Manual of Mental Disorders*. 4th ed. Washington, D.C.: American Psychiatric Association, 1995.

Andre, Rae. *Positive Solitude*. New York: HarperCollins Publishers, 1991.

Bancroft, Anne. *Twentieth-Century Mystics and Sages*. London: Penguin Group, 1989.

Baumgartner, Susan. *My Walden: Tales from Dead Cow Gulch*. Freedom, Calif.: The Crossing Press, 1992.

Bender, Sue. *Plain and Simple: A Woman's Journey to the Amish*. San Francisco: Harper & Row Publishers, 1989.

Berger, Peter L. *Sociology: A Humanistic Perspective*. New York: Anchor Books, 1990.

Bode, Richard. *Beachcombing at Miramar*. New York: Warner Books, 1996.

Burns, David D. *The Feeling Good Handbook*. New York: William Morrow & Co., Inc., 1989.

Cadish, Barry. *Damn! Reflections on Life's Biggest Regrets*. New York: Andrews McMeel Publishing, 2001.

Callahan, Steven. *Adrift: Seventy-Six Days Lost at Sea*. Boston: Houghton Mifflin Co., 1986.

Coleridge, Samuel Taylor. *Poems of Samuel Taylor Coleridge*. New York: Thomas Y. Crowell Co., 1967.

Cooper, David A. *Entering the Sacred Mountain*. New York: Bell Tower, 1994.

Csikszentmimalyi, Mihaly. *The Psychology of Optimal Experience*. New York: Harper & Row Publishers, 1990.

Cunningham, Lawrence S. *The Catholic Heritage*. New York: Crossroad, 1972.

D'Aboville, Gerard. *Alone*. New York: Arcade Publishing, 1993.

De Mello, Anthony. *The Way to Love*. New York: Doubleday, 1992.

Dillard, Annie. *Pilgrim at Tinker Creek*. New York: Harper & Row Publishers, 1974.

Dowrick, Stephanie. *Intimacy and Solitude*. New York: W. W. Norton & Co., 1981.

Dunne, John S. *The Reasons of the Heart*. Macmillan Publishing Co., Inc., 1978.

Elgin, Duane. *Voluntary Simplicity*. New York: William Morrow and Co., Inc., 1981.

Eliot, T. S. *T. S. Eliot: Collected Poems 1909–1962*. New York: Harcourt, Brace & World, 1963.

Ericsson, Stephanie. *Companion Through the Darkness*. New York: HarperCollins Publishers, 1993.

Erskine, Helen Worden. *Out of This World*. New York: G. P. Putnam's Sons, 1953.

Friday, Nancy. *Women on Top*. New York: Simon & Schuster, 1991.

Friedan, Betty. *The Fountain of Age*. New York: Simon & Schuster, 1993.

Fromm, Pete. *Indian Creek Chronicles*. New York: St. Martin's Press, 1993.

Fromm, Pete. *Indian Creek Chronicles*. New York: St. Martin's Press, 1993.

Gardner, Sean. *Missionary*. New York: 1stBooks, 2001.

Gilman, Dorothy. *A New Kind of Country*. (New York: Fawcett Crest, 1978.

Goldenson, Robert M., and Kenneth N. Anderson. *Sex A to Z*. New York: World Almanac, 1989.

Griffin, Susan. *A Chorus of Stones*. New York: Doubleday, 1992.

Gustafson, Jane. *Celibate Passion*. New York: Harper & Row Publishers, 1978.

Halpern, Sue. *Migrations to Solitude*. New York: Pantheon Books, 1992.

Hanh, Thich Nhat. *The Miracle of Mindfulness*. Boston: Beacon Press, 1987.

———. *Peace Is Every Step*. New York: Bantam Books, 1992.

Holland, Barbara. *One's Company*. New York: Ballantine Books, 1992.

Janus, Cynthia L. *The Janus Report on Sexual Behavior*. New York: John Wiley & Sons, Inc., 1993.

Karper, Karen. *Where God Begins to Be*. Grand Rapids, Mich.: William B. Eerdmans Publishing Co., 1994.

Kelly, Marcia, and Jack Kelly. *Sanctuaries*. New York: Harmony Books, 1993.

Koller, Alice. *The Stations of Solitude*. New York: Morrow, 1990.

Kottler, Jeffrey. *Private Moments, Secret Selves*. Los Angeles: Jeremy P. Tarcher, Inc., 1990.

Lapham, Lewis H. *Money and Class in America*. New York: Ballantine Books, 1989.

Lax, Eric. *Woody Allen*. New York: Alfred A. Knopf, 1991.

L'Engle, Madeleine. *A Circle of Quiet*. New York: Farrar, Straus and Giroux, 1972.

Leslie, Edward E. *Desperate Journeys, Abandoned Souls*. Boston: Houghton Mifflin Co., 1988.

Lindbergh, Anne Morrow. *Gift from the Sea*. New York: Vintage Books, 1991.

Masters, William H., and Virgina E. Johnson. *Human Sexual Response*. Boston: Little, Brown and Co., 1966.

McCall, Edith. *Sometimes We Dance Alone*. Thorndike, Maine: G. K. Hall & Co., 1994.

Merton, Thomas. *Thoughts In Solitude*. New York: Farrar, Straus & Cudahy, 1958.

Mookerjee, Ajit, and Madhu Khanna. *The Tantric Way*. Boston: New York Graphic Society, 1977.

Moore, Brian. *The Lonely Passion of Judith Hearne*. Boston: Little, Brown and Co., 1955.

Moustakas, Clark E. *Loneliness and Love*. New York: Prentice Hall Press, 1991.

Nelson, Richard. *The Island Within*. New York: Vintage Books, 1991.

Nomura, Yushi. *Desert Wisdom*. New York: Doubleday & Co., Inc., 1982.

Norris, Kathleen. *Dakota: A Spiritual Journey*. New York: Houghton Mifflin Co., 1993).

Olson, Sigmund. *Reflections from the North Country*. New York: Alfred A. Knopf, 1976.

Orem, Sara, and Larry Demarest. *Living Simply*. (Deerfield Beach, Fla.: Health Communications, Inc., 1994.

Palmer, Greg. *Death: The Trip of a Lifetime*. San Francisco: HarperSanFrancisco, 1993.

Patterson, Richard B. *Becoming a Modern Contemplative*. Chicago: Loyola University Press, 1995.

Peck, M. Scott. *The Road Less Traveled*. New York: Simon & Schuster, 1978.

Perkins, Robert. *Into the Great Solitude*. Henry Holt and Co., 1991.

Richards, Judith. *The Sounds of Silence*. New York: Putnam, 1977.

Richards, Mary Caroline. *Centering in Pottery, Poetry, and the Person*. Middletown, Conn.: Wesleyan University Press, 1989.

Rinpoche, Sogyal. *The Tibetan Book of Living and Dying*. San Francisco: HarperCollins, 1992.

Roskolenko, Harry, ed. *Solo.*Chicago: Playboy Press, 1973.

Roth, Philip. *Portnoy's Complaint.* New York: Random House, 1967.

Russianoff, Penelope. *Why Do I Think I Am Nothing Without a Man?* New York: Bantam Books, 1982.

Sallis, James. *Renderings.* Seattle: Black Heron Press, 1995.

Sarton, May. *The House by the Sea.* Boston: G. K. Hall & Co., 1977.

———. *Journal of a Solitude.* New York: W. W. Norton & Co., 1973.

———. *The Silence Now.* New York: W. W. Norton & Co., 1988.

Scot, Barbara J. *Prairie Reunion.* New York: Farrar, Straus and Giroux, 1995.

———. *The Violet Shyness of Their Eyes.* Corvallis, Ore.: Calyx Books, 1993.

Seferis, George. "Summer Solstice." In *The Antaeus Anthology*, edited by Daniel Halpern. New York: Bantam Books, 1986.

Shannon-Thornberry, Milo. *The Alternate Celebrations Catalogue.* New York: The Pilgrim Press, 1982.

Sheehan, George. *Going the Distance.* New York: Villard, 1996.

Shi, David E. *The Simple Life.* New York: Oxford University Press, 1985.

Shulman, Alix Kates. *Drinking the Rain.* New York: Farrar, Straus and Giroux, 1995.

Siebert, Al. *The Survivor Personality.* Portland, Ore.: Practical Psychology Press, 1993.

Sinetar, Marsha. *Ordinary People as Monks and Mystics.* Mahway, N.J.: Paulist Press, 1986.

Slocum, Joshua. *Sailing Alone Around the World.* London: Century Publishing, 1984.

Smith, Don Ian. *Wild Rivers and Mountain Trails*. Nashville, Tenn.: Abingdon Press, 1972.

Steindl-Rast, David, with Sharon Lebell. *The Music of Silence*. San Francisco: HarperCollins, 1995.

St. James, Elaine. *Simplify Your Life*. New York: Hyperion, 1994.

Stoddard, Alexandra. *Living a Beautiful Life*. New York: Random House, 1986.

Storr, Anthony. *Solitude: A Return to the Self*. New York: The Free Press, 1988.

Talbot, John Michael. *Hermitage*. New York: Crossroad, 1989.

Thoreau, Henry David. *Three Complete Books*. New York: Gramercy Books, 1993.

Walker, Susan, ed. *Speaking of Silence*. New York: Paulist Press, 1987.

Warren, Ann K. *Anchorites and Their Patrons in Medieval England*. Berkeley: University of California Press, 1985.

Watts, Alan. *The Book: On the Taboo Against Knowing Who You Are*. New York: Pantheon Books, 1966.

Winokur, Jon, comp. and ed. *The Portable Curmudgeon*. New York: New American Library, 1987.

Younghusband, Francis. *Modern Mystics*. New York: E. P. Dutton & Co., Inc., 1935.

Yount, John. *Toots In Solitude*. New York: St. Martin's/Marek, 1984.

Other Books from Beyond Words Publishing, Inc.

Our Turn, Our Time
Women Truly Coming of Age
Editor: Cynthia Black; Foreword: Christina Baldwin
$14.95, softcover

Our Turn, Our Time is an amazing collection of essays written by women who are committed to celebrating and valuing their passages into the second half of life. These women are redefining the role older women play in contemporary society by embracing creativity, spirituality, and sisterhood. These essays are filled with insight, humor, and compassion on a broad variety of topics: the richness of women's groups, the rewards of volunteering, the power of crone ceremonies, the fires of creative expression, the challenges of a changing body, and the confidence that comes from success in later life.

Rites of Passage
Celebrating Life's Changes
Authors: Kathleen Wall, Ph.D., and Gary Ferguson
$12.95, softcover

Every major transition in our lives—be it marriage, high-school graduation, the death of a parent or spouse, or the last child leaving home—brings with it opportunities for growth and self-actualization and for repositioning ourselves in the world. Personal ritual—the focus of *Rites of Passage*—allows us to use the energy held within the anxiety of change to nourish the new person that is forever struggling to be born. *Rites of Passage* begins by explaining to readers that human growth is not linear, as many of us assume, but rather occurs in a five-part cycle. After sharing the patterns of transition, the authors then show the reader how ritual can help him or her move through these specific life changes: work and career, intimate relationships, friends, divorce, changes within the family, adolescence, issues in the last half of life, and personal loss.

When God Winks

How the Power of Concidence Guides Your Life
Author: SQuire Rushnell
$16.95, hardcover

When God Winks confirms a belief secretly held by most readers: there is more to coincidences than meets the eye. Like winks from a loving grandparent, coincidences are messages from above that you are not alone and everything will be OK. This compelling theory of why coincidences exist is applied to fascinating stories in history, sports, the news, medicine, and relationships involving both everyday people and celebrities.

The Woman's Book of Dreams

Dreaming as a Spiritual Practice
Author: Connie Cockrell Kaplan; Foreword: Jamie Sams
$14.95, softcover

Dreams are the windows to your future and the catalysts to bringing the new and creative into your life. Everyone dreams. Understanding the power of dreaming helps you achieve your greatest potential with ease. *The Woman's Book of Dreams* emphasizes the uniqueness of women's dreaming and shows the reader how to dream with intention, clarity, and focus. In addition, this book will teach you how to recognize the thirteen types of dreams, how your monthly cycles affect your dreaming, how the moon's position in the sky and its relationship to your astrological chart determine your dreaming, and how to track your dreams and create a personal map of your dreaming patterns. Connie Kaplan guides you through an ancient woman's group form called dream circle—a sacred space in which to share dreams with others on a regular basis. Dream circle allows you to experience life's mystery by connecting with other dreamers. It shows you that through dreaming together with your circle, you create the reality in which you live. It is time for you to recognize the power of dreams and to put yours into action. This book will inspire you to do all that—and more.

The Intuitive Way

A Guide to Living from Inner Wisdom
Author: Penney Peirce; Foreword: Carol Adrienne
$16.95, softcover

When intuition is in full bloom, life takes on a magical, effortless quality; your world is suddenly full of synchronicities, creative insights, and abundant knowledge just for the asking. *The Intuitive Way* shows you how to enter that state of perceptual aliveness and integrate it into daily life to achieve greater natural flow through an easy-to-understand, ten-step course. Author Penney Peirce synthesizes teachings from psychology, East-West philosophy, religion, metaphysics, and business. In simple and direct language, Peirce describes the intuitive process as a new way of life and demonstrates many practical lapplications from speeding decision-making to expanding personal growth. Whether you're just beginning to search for a richer, fuller life experience or are looking for more subtle, sophisticated insights about your spiritual path, *The Intuitive Way* will be your companion as you progress through the stages of intuition development.

Teach Only Love

The Twelve Principles of Attitudinal Healing
Author: Gerald G. Jampolsky, M.D.
$12.95, softcover

From best-selling author Dr. Gerald Jampolsky comes a revised and expanded version of one of his classic works, based on *A Course in Miracles*. In 1975, Dr. Jampolsky founded the Center for Attitudinal Healing, a place where children and adults with life-threatening illnesses could practice peace of mind as an instrument of spiritual transformation and inner healing—practices that soon evolved into an approach to life with profound benefits for everyone. This book explains the twelve principles developed at the Center, all of which are based on the healing power of love, forgiveness, and oneness. They provide a powerful guide that allows all of us to heal our relationships and bring peace and harmony to every aspect of our lives.

Forgiveness

The Greatest Healer of All
Author: Gerald G. Jampolsky, M.D.; Foreword: Neale Donald Walsch
$12.95, softcover

Forgiveness: The Greatest Healer of All is written in simple, down-to-earth language. It explains why so many of us find it difficult to forgive and why holding on to grievances is really a decision to suffer. The book describes what causes us to be unforgiving and how our minds work to justify this. It goes on to point out the toxic side effects of being unforgiving and the havoc it can play on our bodies and on our lives. But above all, it leads us to the vast benefits of forgiving.

The author shares powerful stories that open our hearts to the miracles which can take place when we truly believe that no one needs to be excluded from our love.

Sprinkled throughout the book are Forgiveness Reminders that may be used as daily affirmations supporting a new life free of past grievances.

Healing Your Rift with God
A Guide to Spiritual Renewal and Ultimate Healing
Author: Paul Sibcy
$14.95, softcover

God, says Paul Sibcy, is everything that is. All of us—faithful seekers or otherwise—have some area of confusion, hurt, or denial around this word, or our personal concept of God, that keeps us from a full expression of our spirituality. *Healing Your Rift with God* is a guidebook for finding our own personal rifts with God and healing them. Sibcy explains the nature of a spiritual rift, how this wound can impair our lives, and how such a wound may be healed by the earnest seeker, with or without help from a counselor or teacher. *Healing Your Rift with God* will also assist those in the helping professions who wish to facilitate what the author calls ultimate healing. The book includes many personal stories from the author's life, teaching, and counseling work, and its warm narrative tone creates an intimate author–reader relationship that inspires the healing process.

Tibetan Wisdom for Western Life
Authors: Joseph Arpaia, M.D., and Lobsang Rapgay, Ph.D.
Foreword: His Holiness the Dalai Lama
$14.95, softcover

By relating meditative practices to specific mental qualities, *Tibetan Wisdom for Western Life* makes meditation a thorough and logical system of personal development. Part I of the book describes the basic practices of centering, attending, concentrating, and opening and how you develop the five mental qualities of Steadiness, Pliancy, Warmth, Clarity, and Spaciousness. Part II describes how to use the practices from Part I to enhance health, performance, relationships, and spirituality in just fifteen minutes per day. The book uses numerous stories and examples of two people, Brian and Maria, to illustrate the techniques. Brian and Maria are amalgams of the hundreds of people the authors have taught, and the inner details of their experience will capture the readers interest and augment the instructions for the techniques. This is above all a practical book, with a philosophical depth that does not inhibit the reader. The techniques presented are based on a profound wisdom that is expressed in purely Western terms. The presentation is secular as well, so that readers of all traditions will be able to benefit.

Seeing Your Life Through New Eyes
InSights to Freedom from Your Past
Authors: Paul Brenner, M.D., Ph.D., and Donna Martin, M.A.
$14.95, softcover

Seeing Your Life Through New Eyes is in a hands-on workbook format that helps you create a diary of self-discovery and assists you in resolving any misunderstood relationships. You can learn how to uncover unconscious patterns that define how you love, what you value, and what unique gifts you have in life. This book reveals those obstacles that too often interfere with loving relationships and creative expression, and it includes diagrams to use for your personal exploration and growth.

To order or to request a catalog, contact

Beyond Words Publishing, Inc.

20827 N.W. Cornell Road, Suite 500

Hillsboro, OR 97124-9808

503-531-8700 or 1-800-284-9673

You can also visit our Web site at www.beyondword.com or e-mail us at info@beyondword.com.

BEYOND WORDS PUBLISHING, INC.

OUR CORPORATE MISSION

Inspire to Integrity

OUR DECLARED VALUES

We give to all of life as life has given us.
We honor all relationships.
Trust and stewardship are integral to fulfilling dreams.
Collaboration is essential to create miracles.
Creativity and aesthetics nourish the soul.
Unlimited thinking is fundamental.
Living your passion is vital.
Joy and humor open our hearts to growth.
It is important to remind ourselves of love.